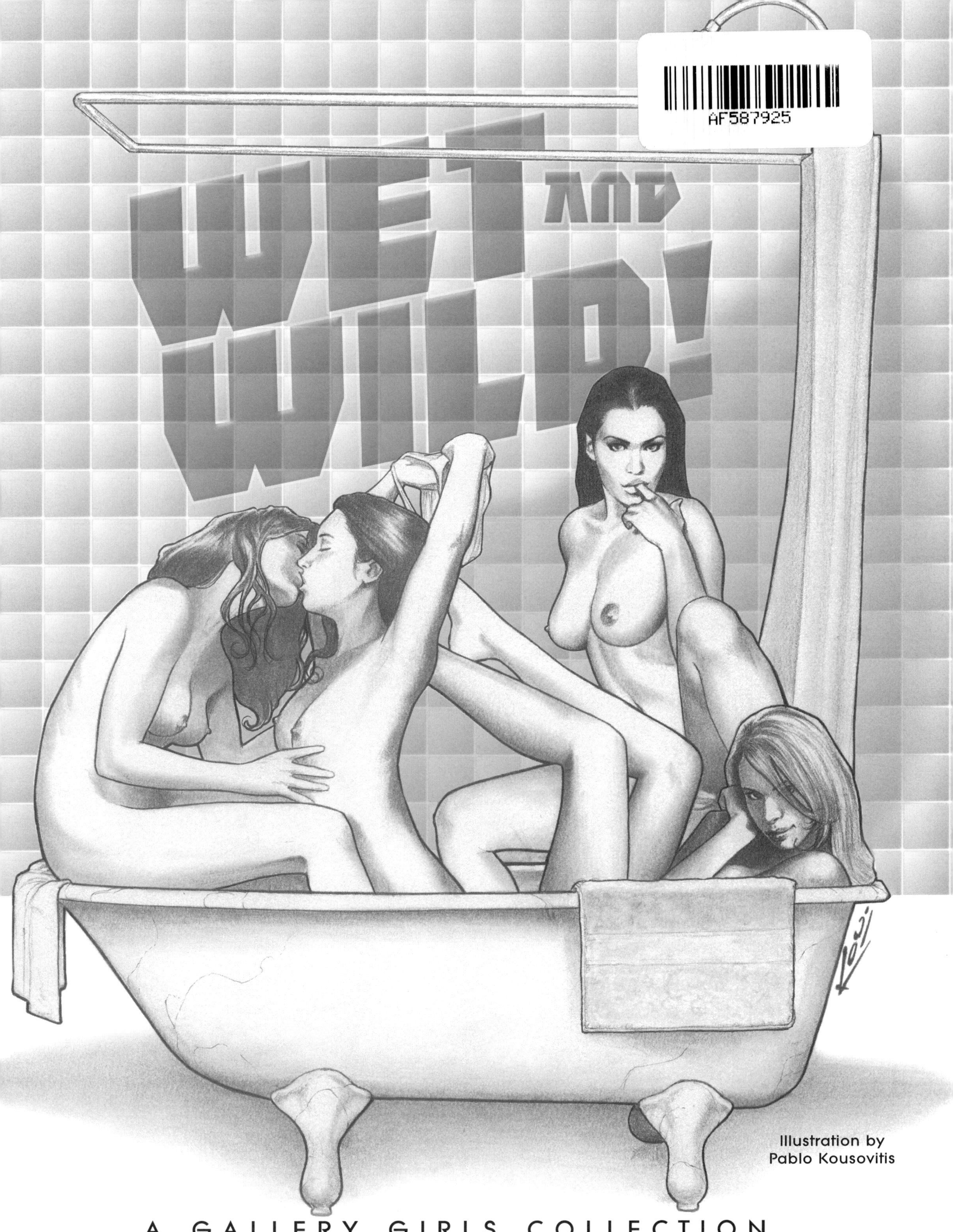

Illustration by
Pablo Kousovitis

A GALLERY GIRLS COLLECTION

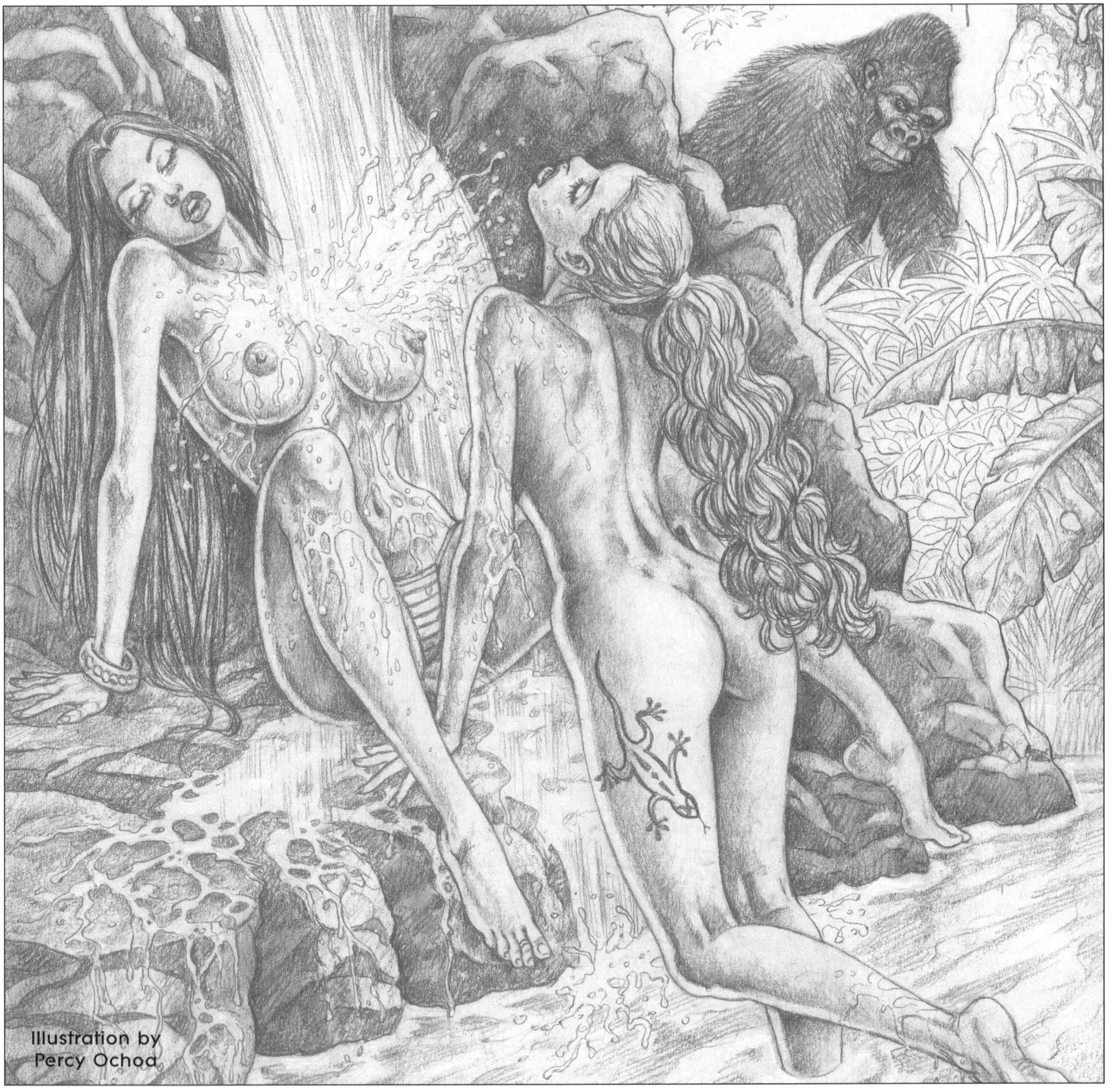

Illustration by
Percy Ochoa

WET AND WILD!

Volume One

Book design by Grassy Knoll Studios.

Published by
SQP Inc.
PO Box 248 - Columbus, NJ 08022

Sal Quartuccio & Bob Keenan - Publishers

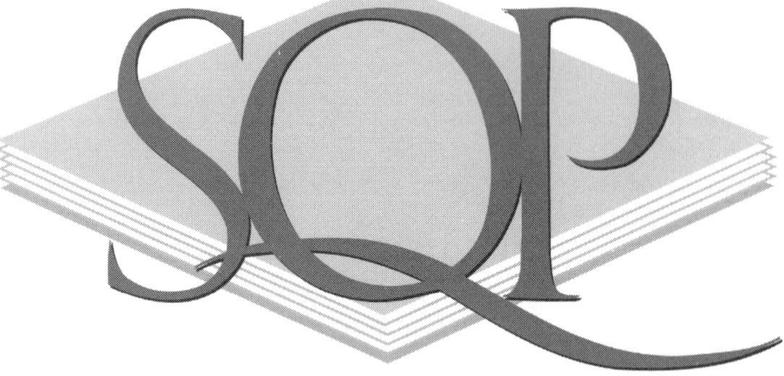

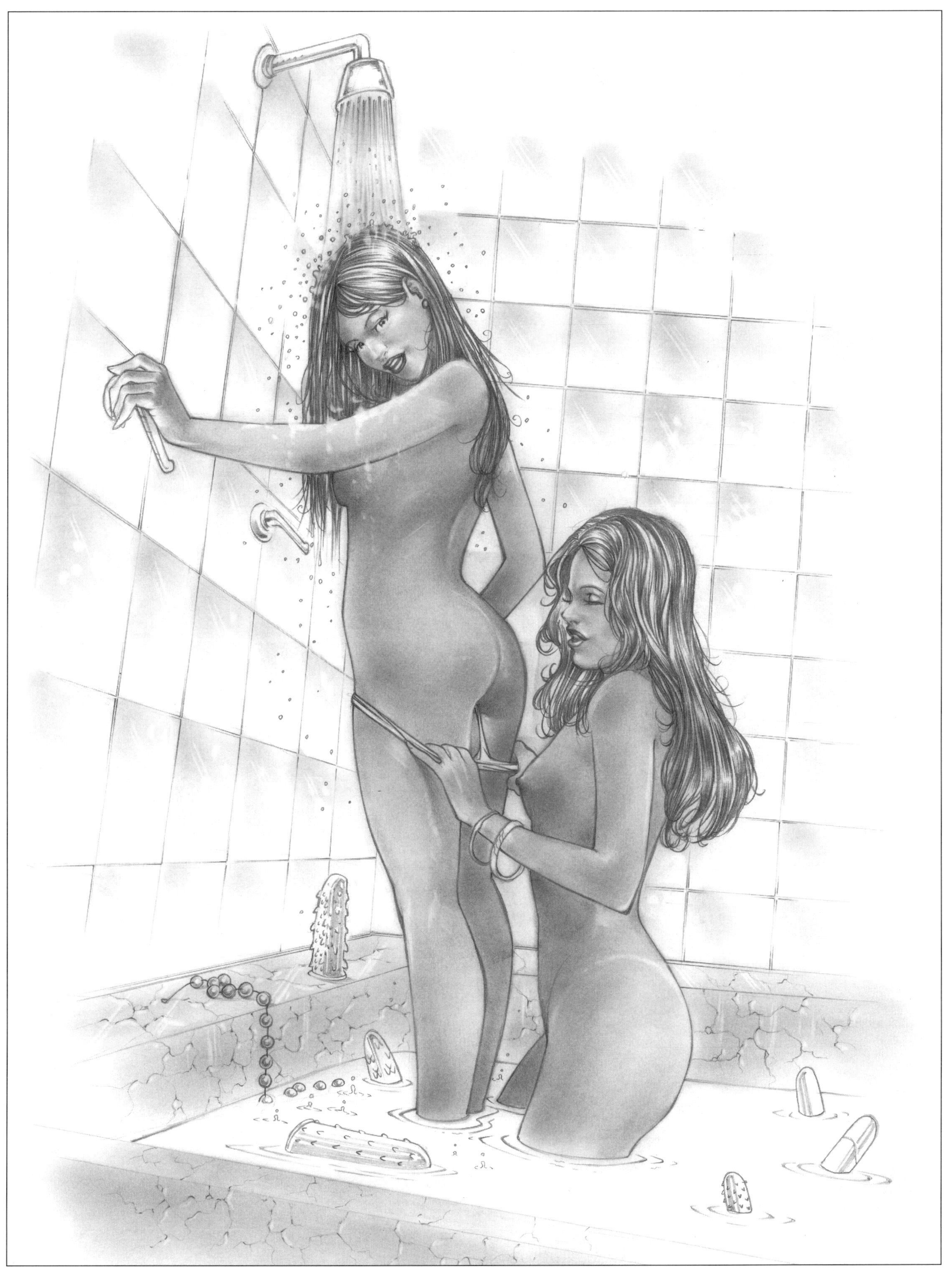

J.L. Czerniawski

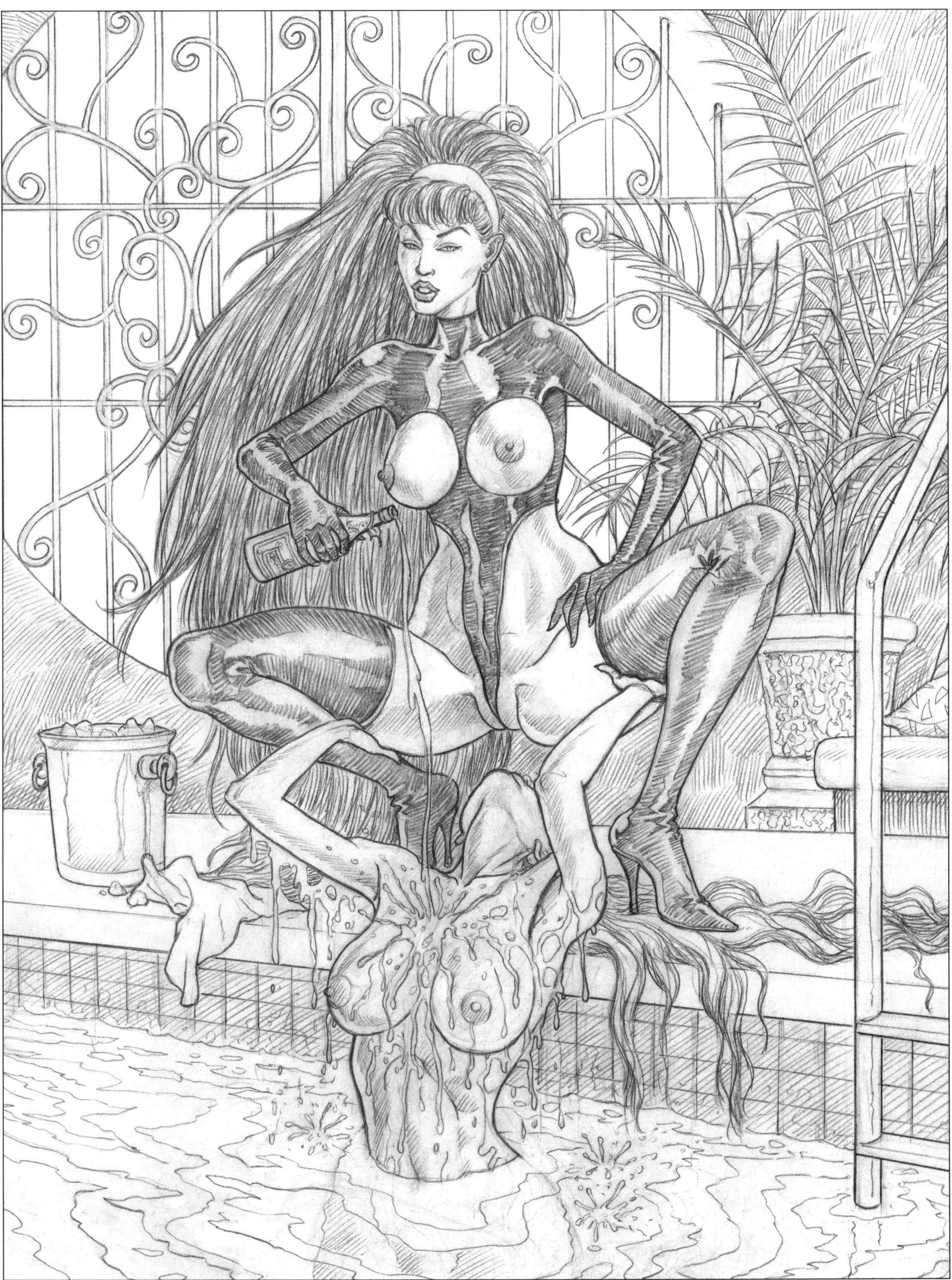

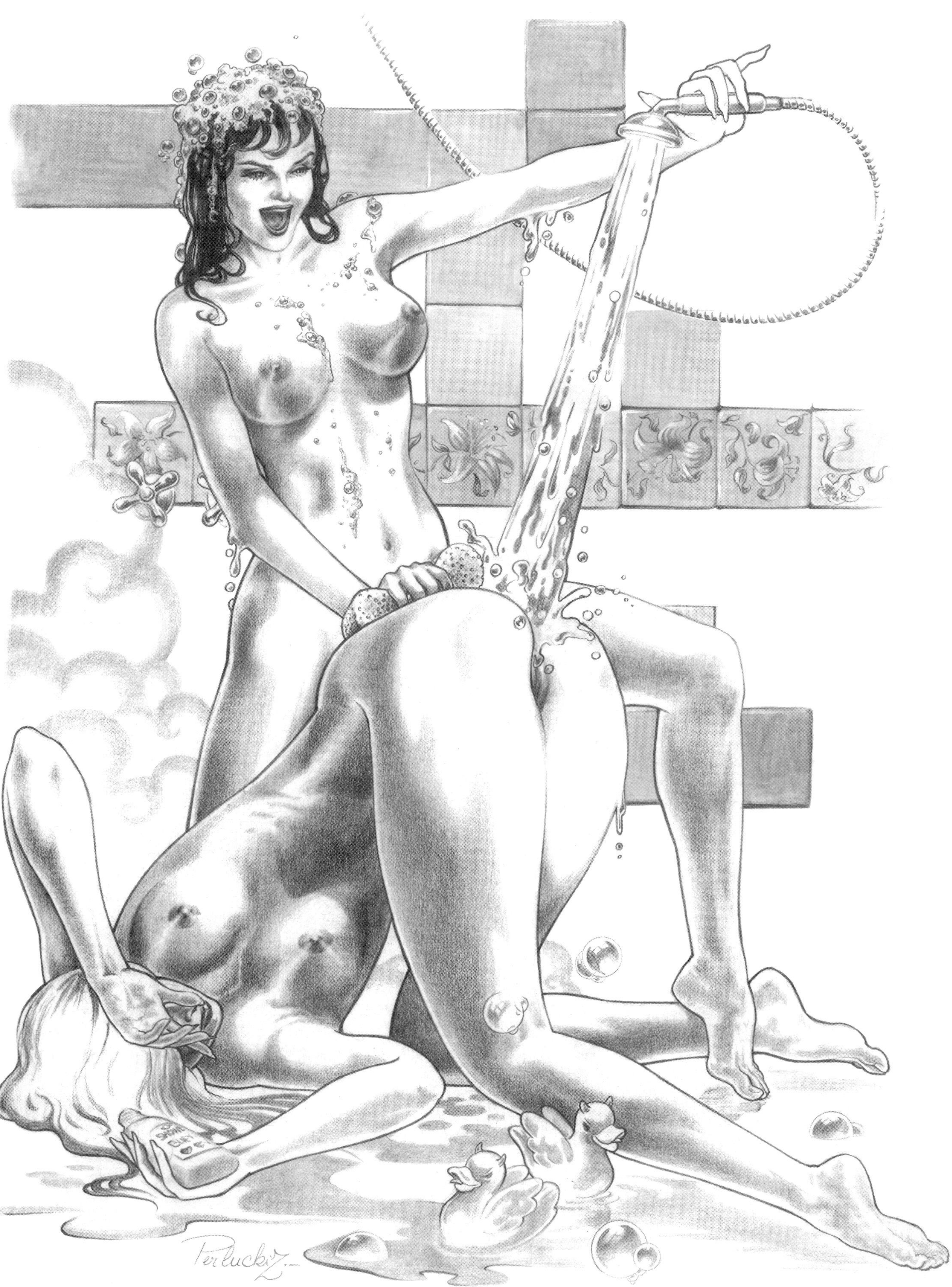

Perla Pilucki

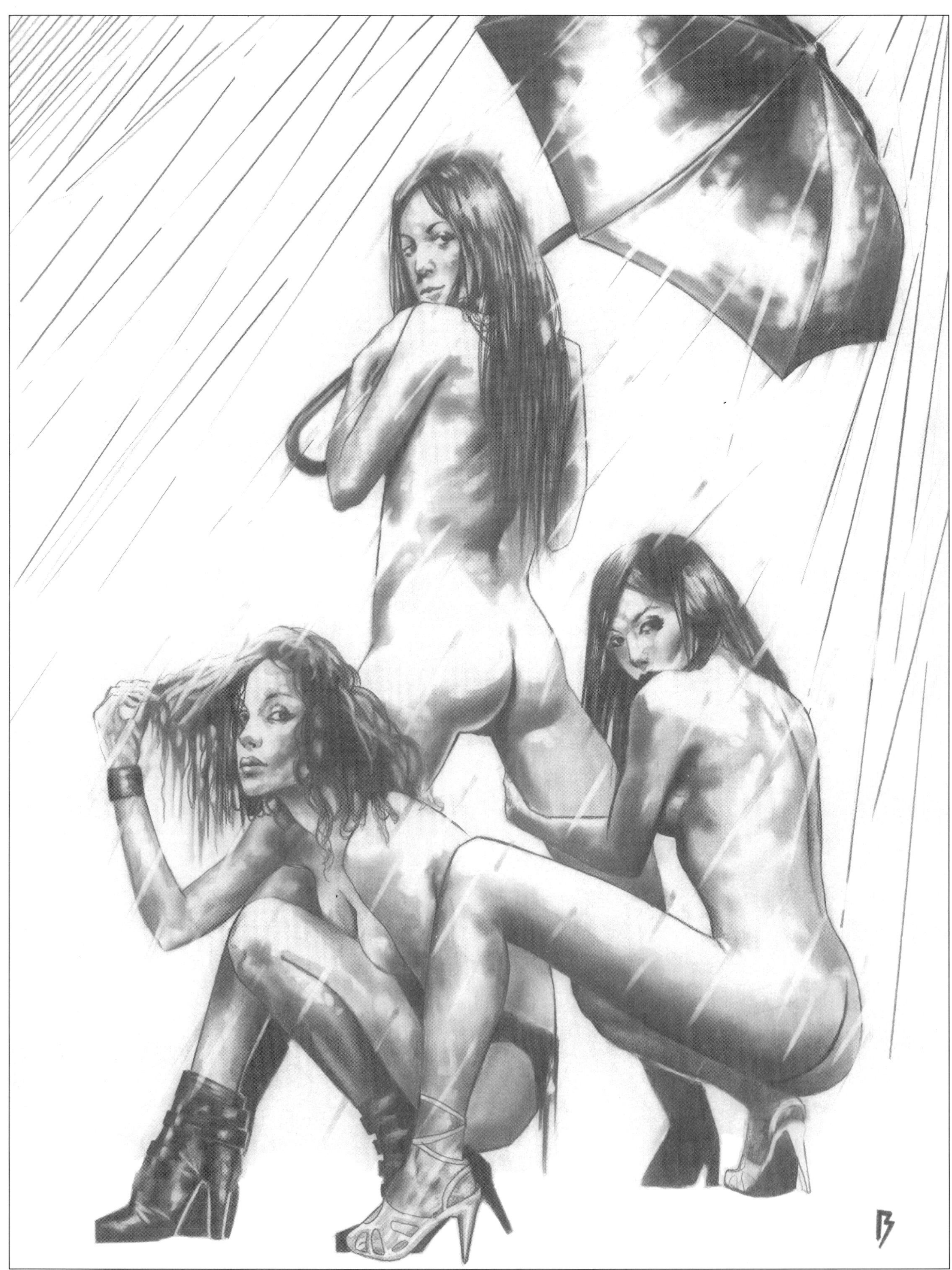

Luis Buci

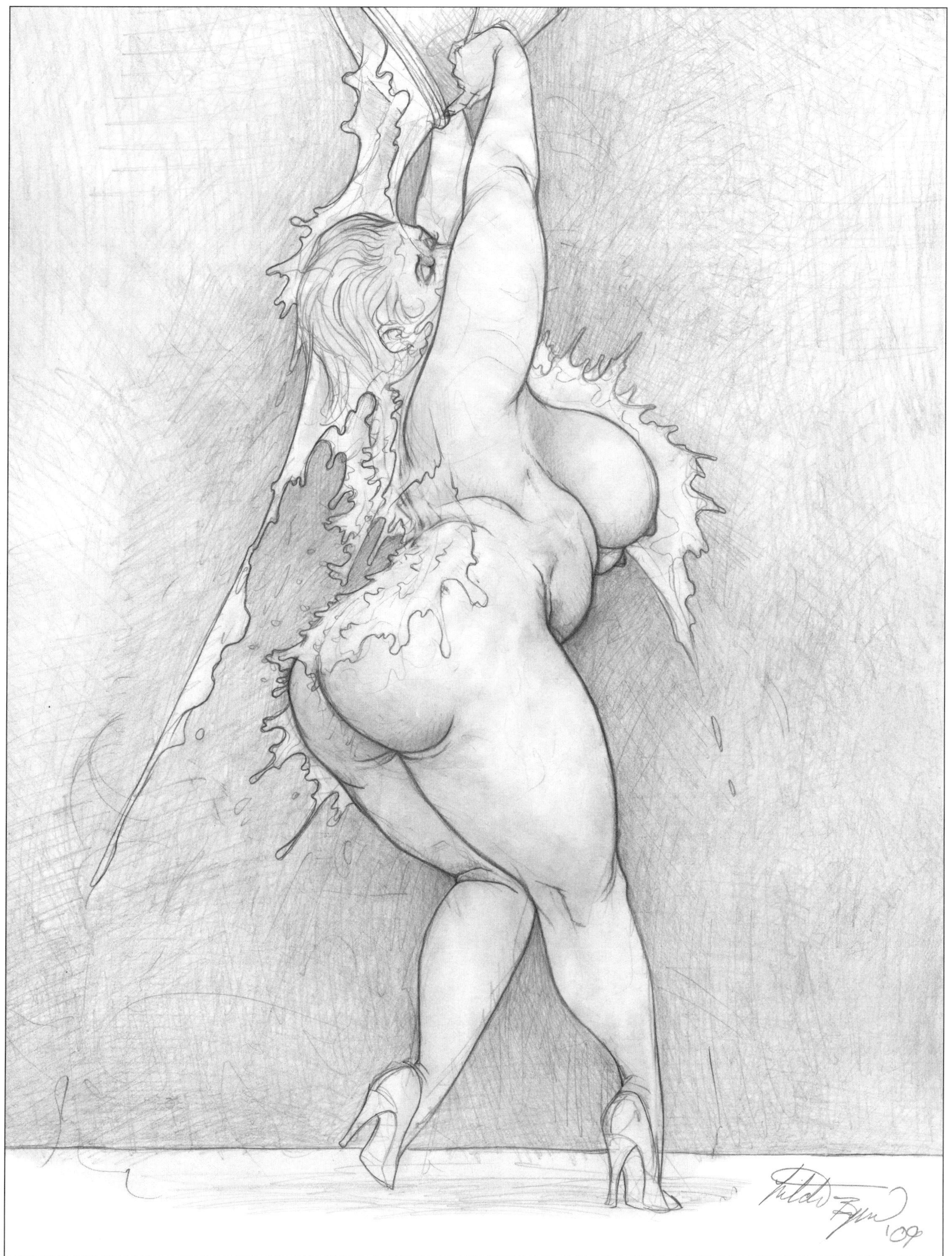

Mitch Byrd

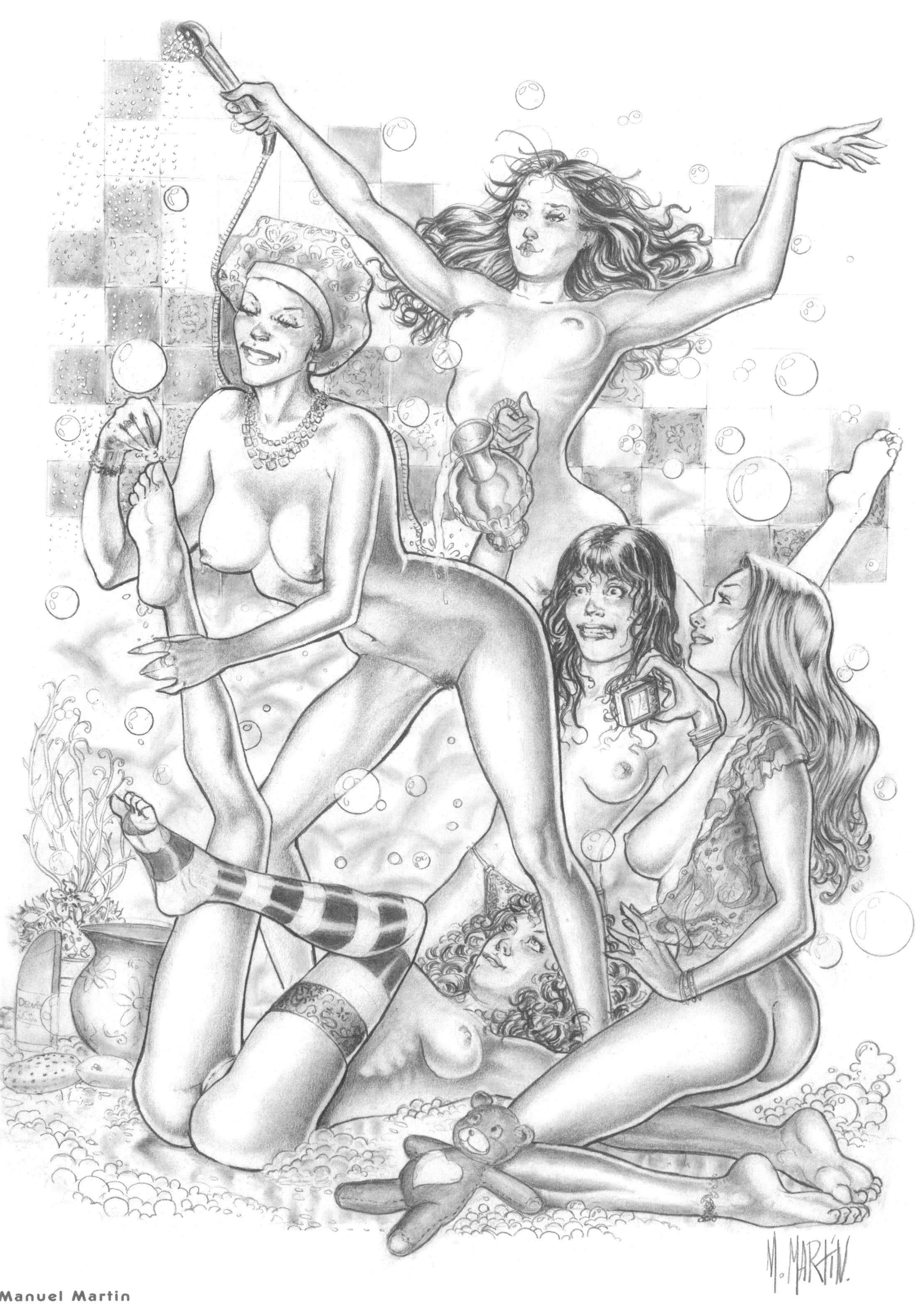

Manuel Martin

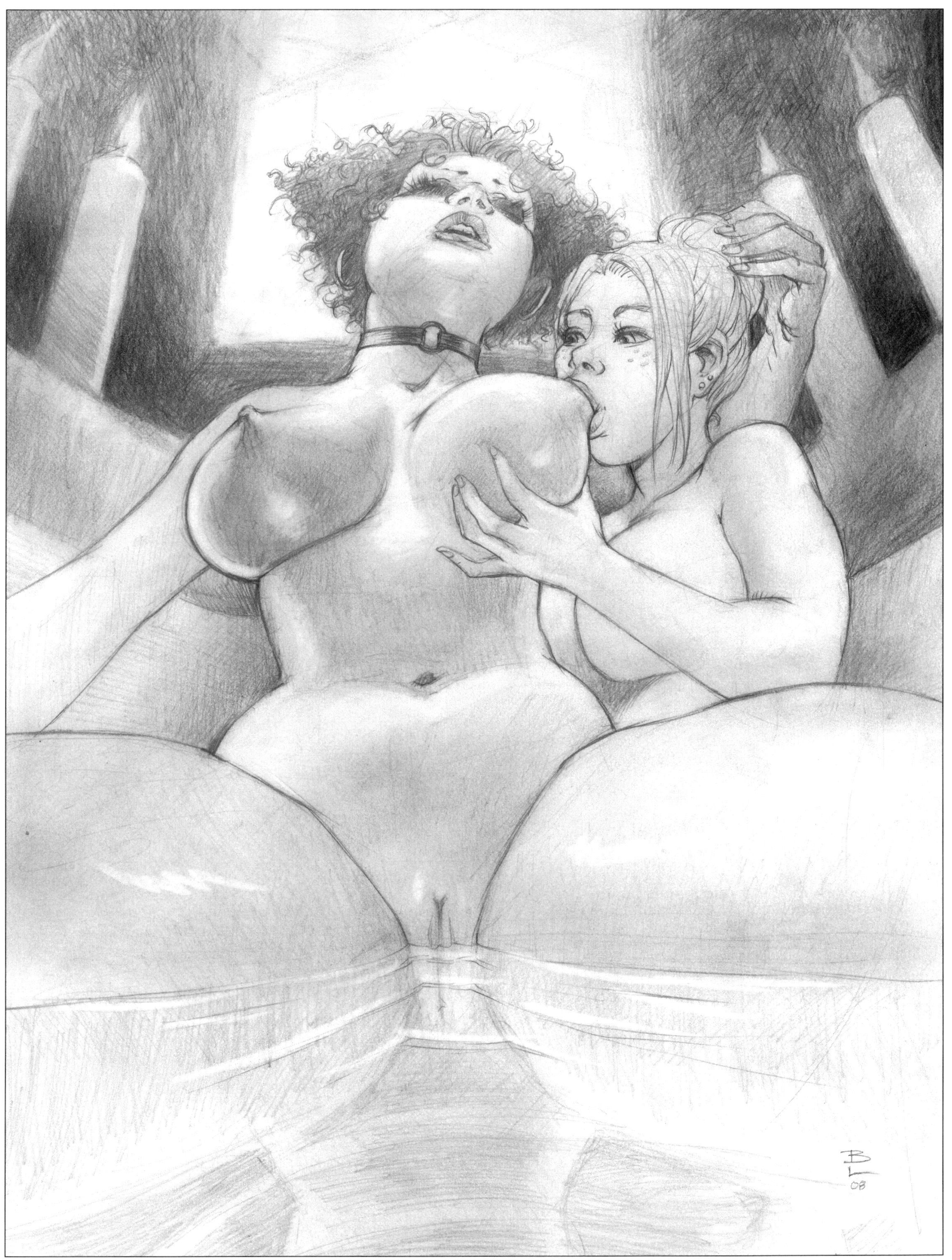

Brian LeBlanc

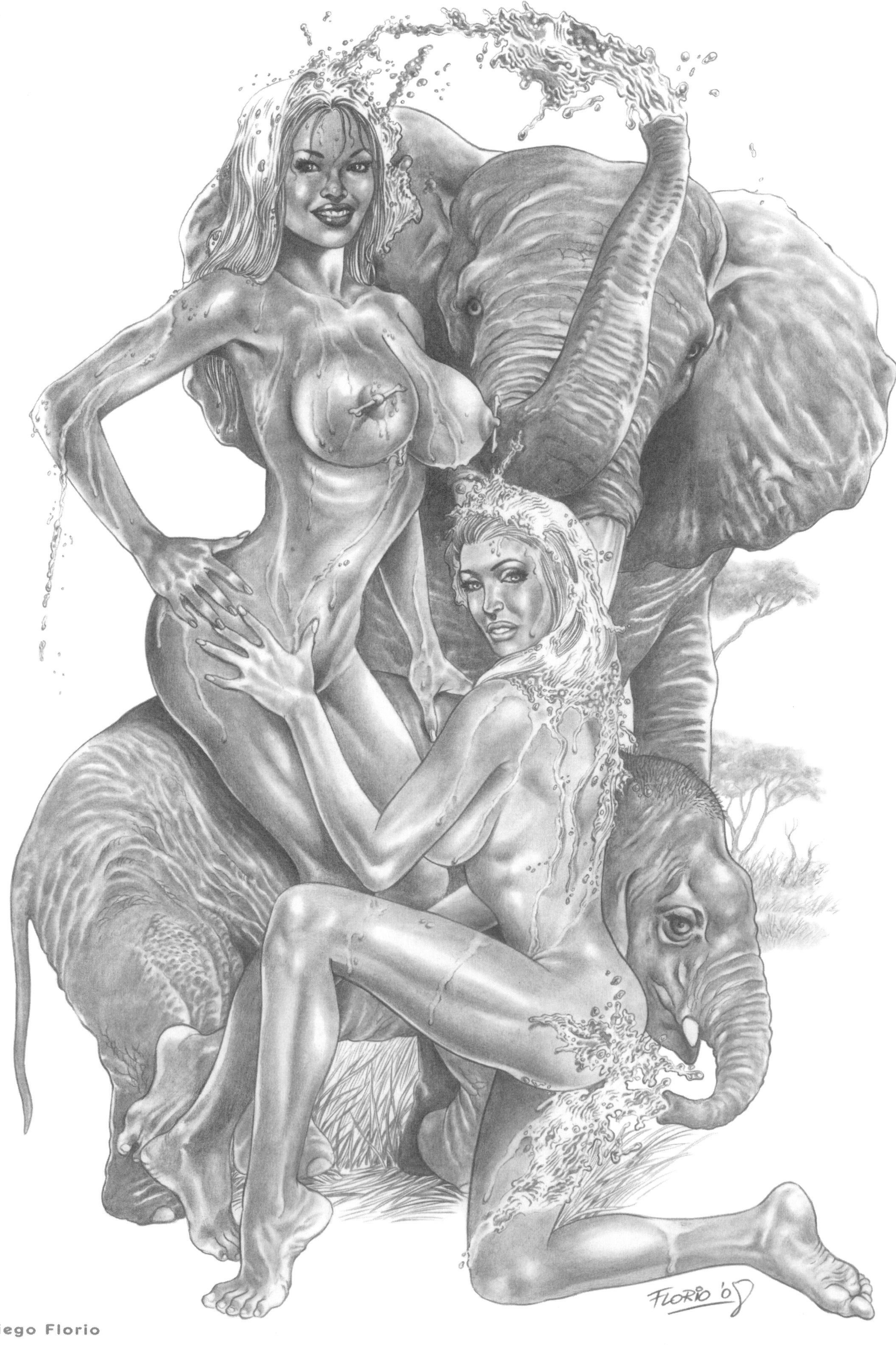

Diego Florio

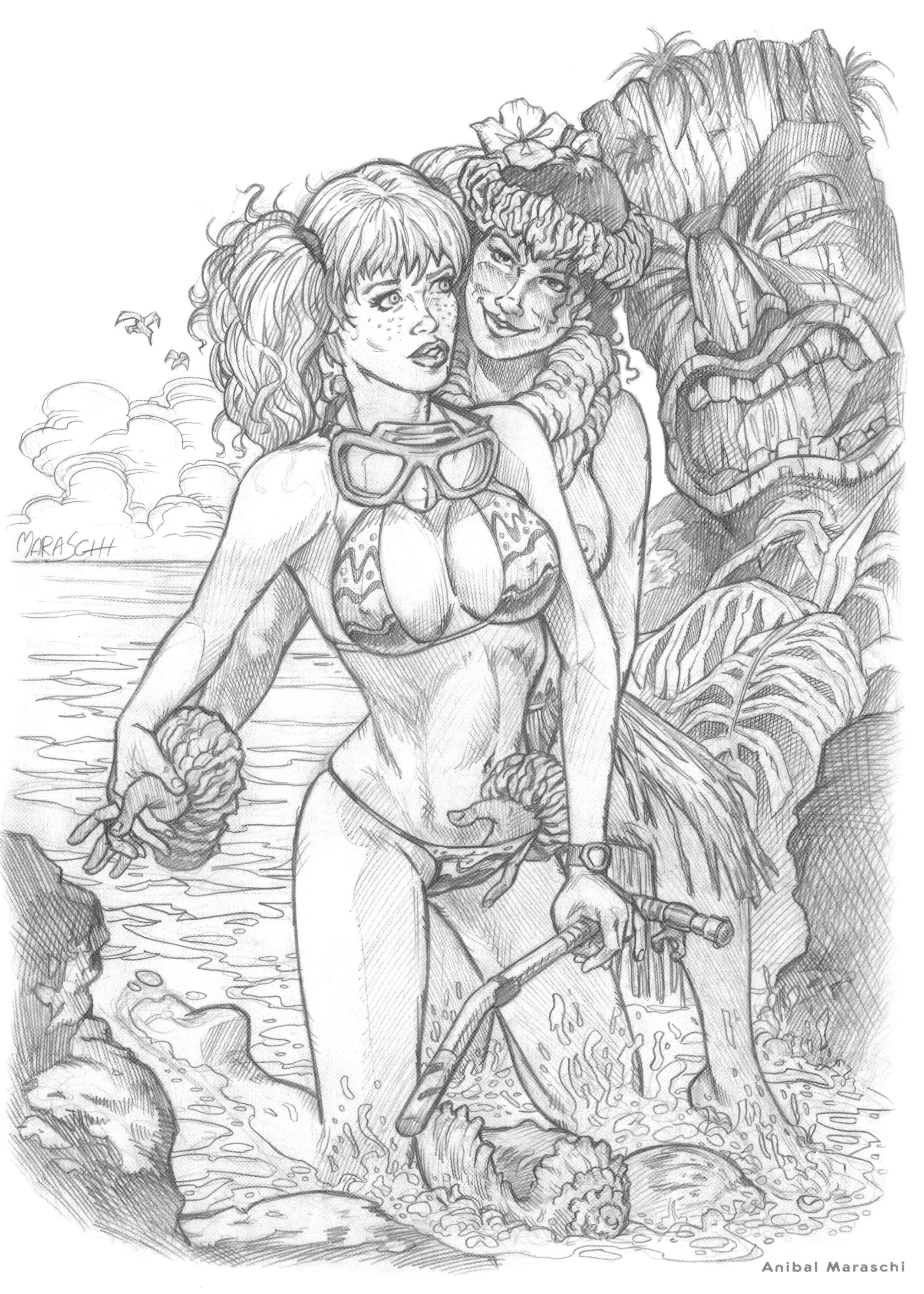

Anibal Maraschi

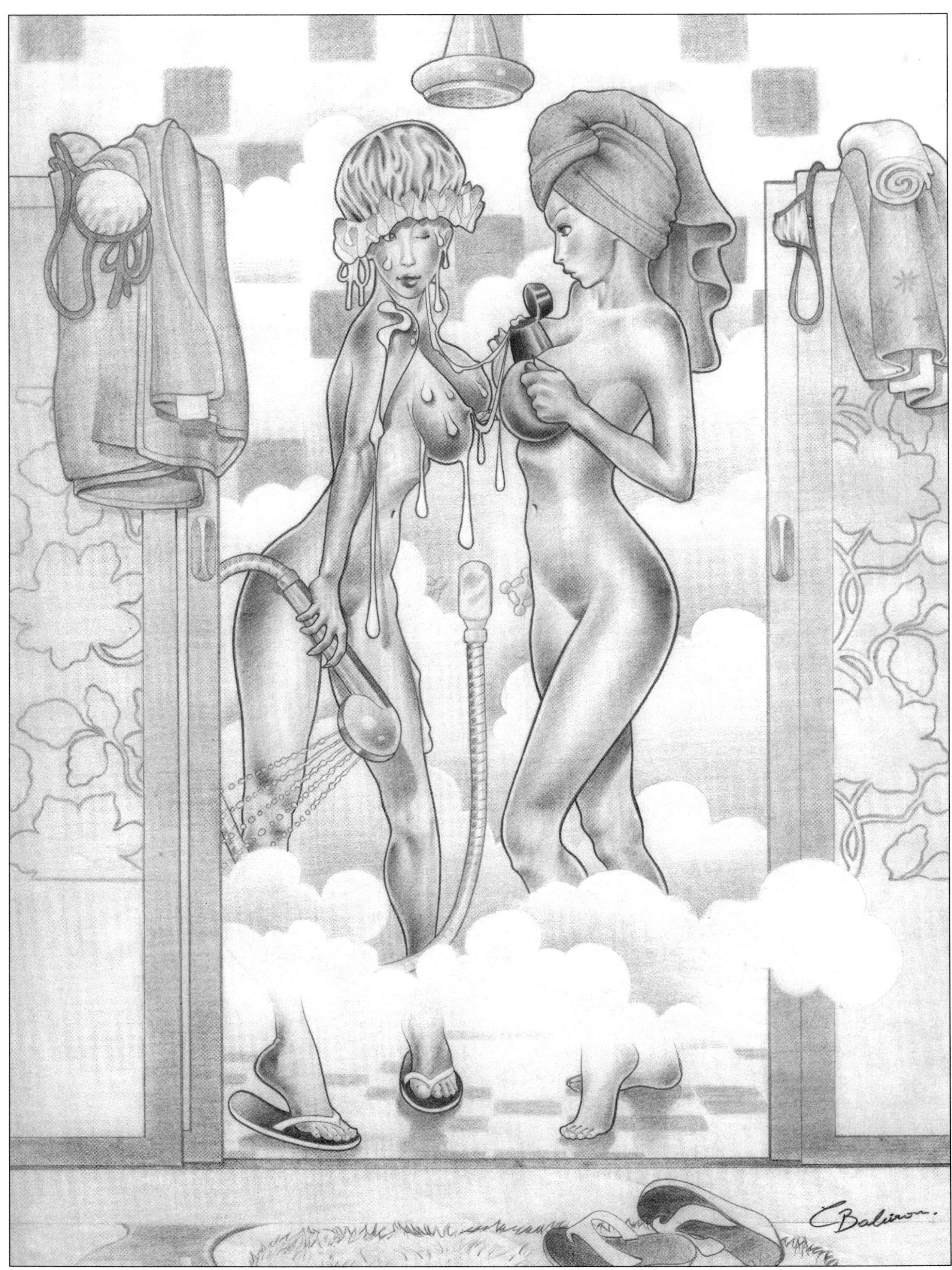

Esteban Baleiron

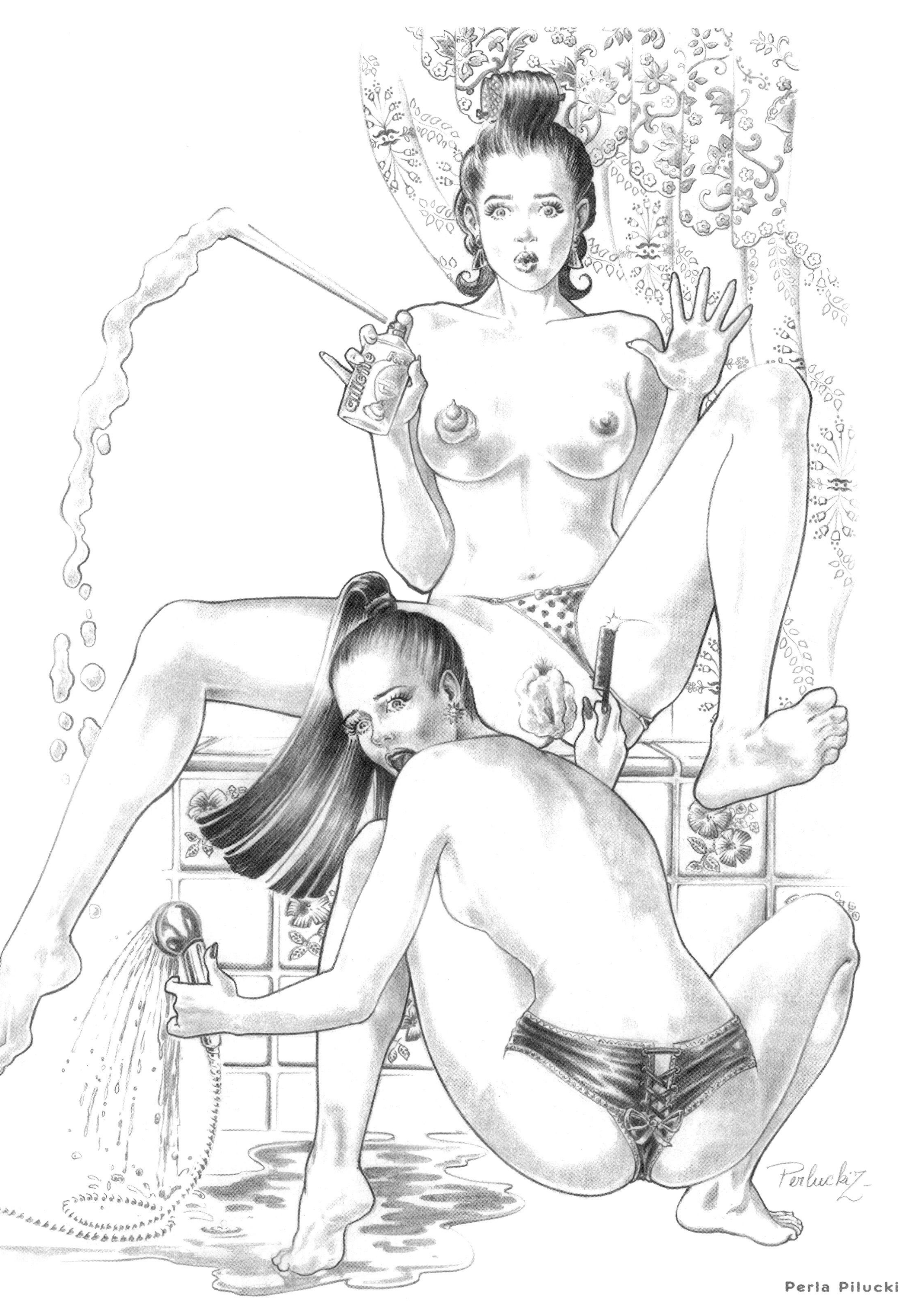

Perla Pilucki

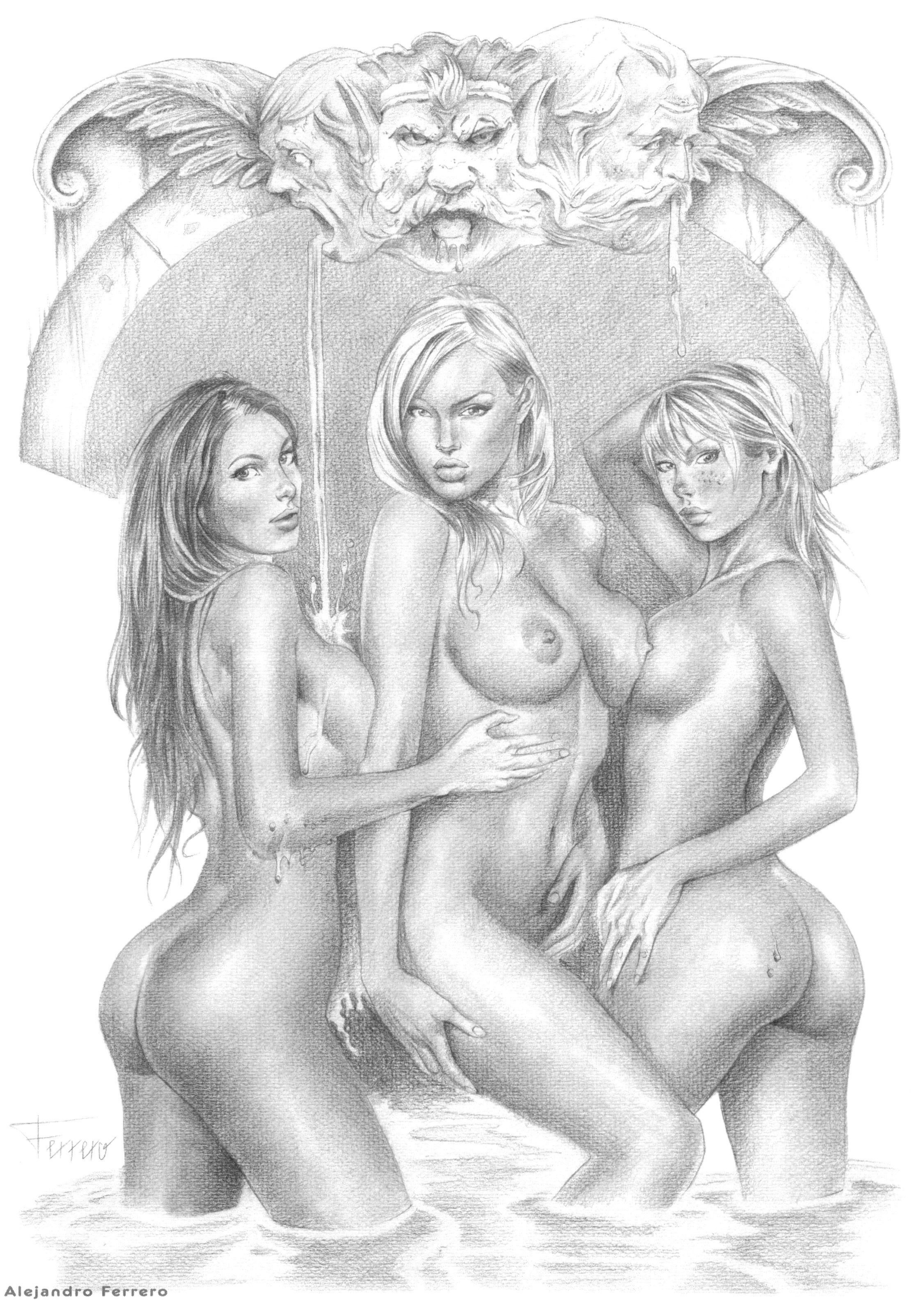

Alejandro Ferrero

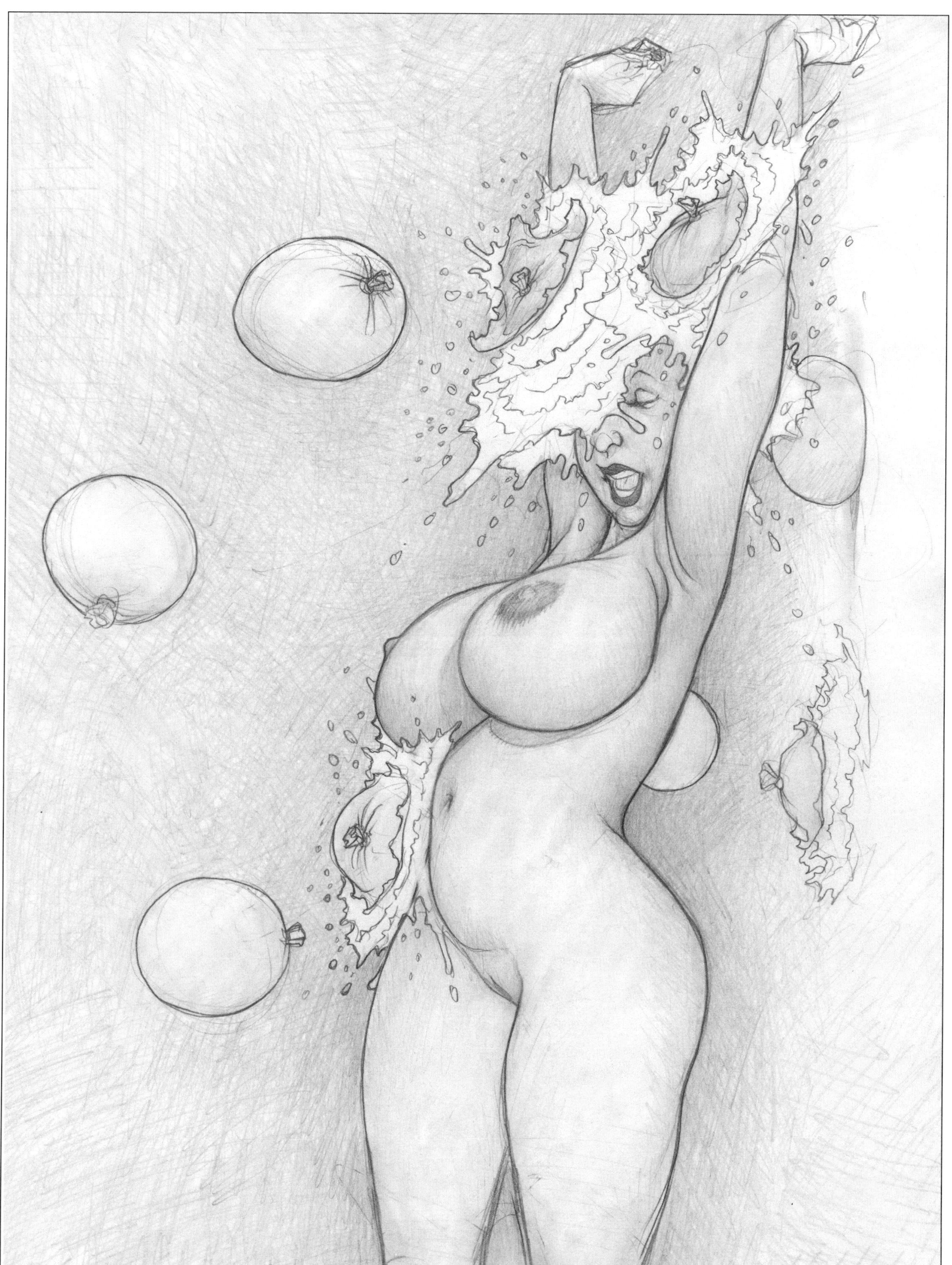

Mitch Byrd

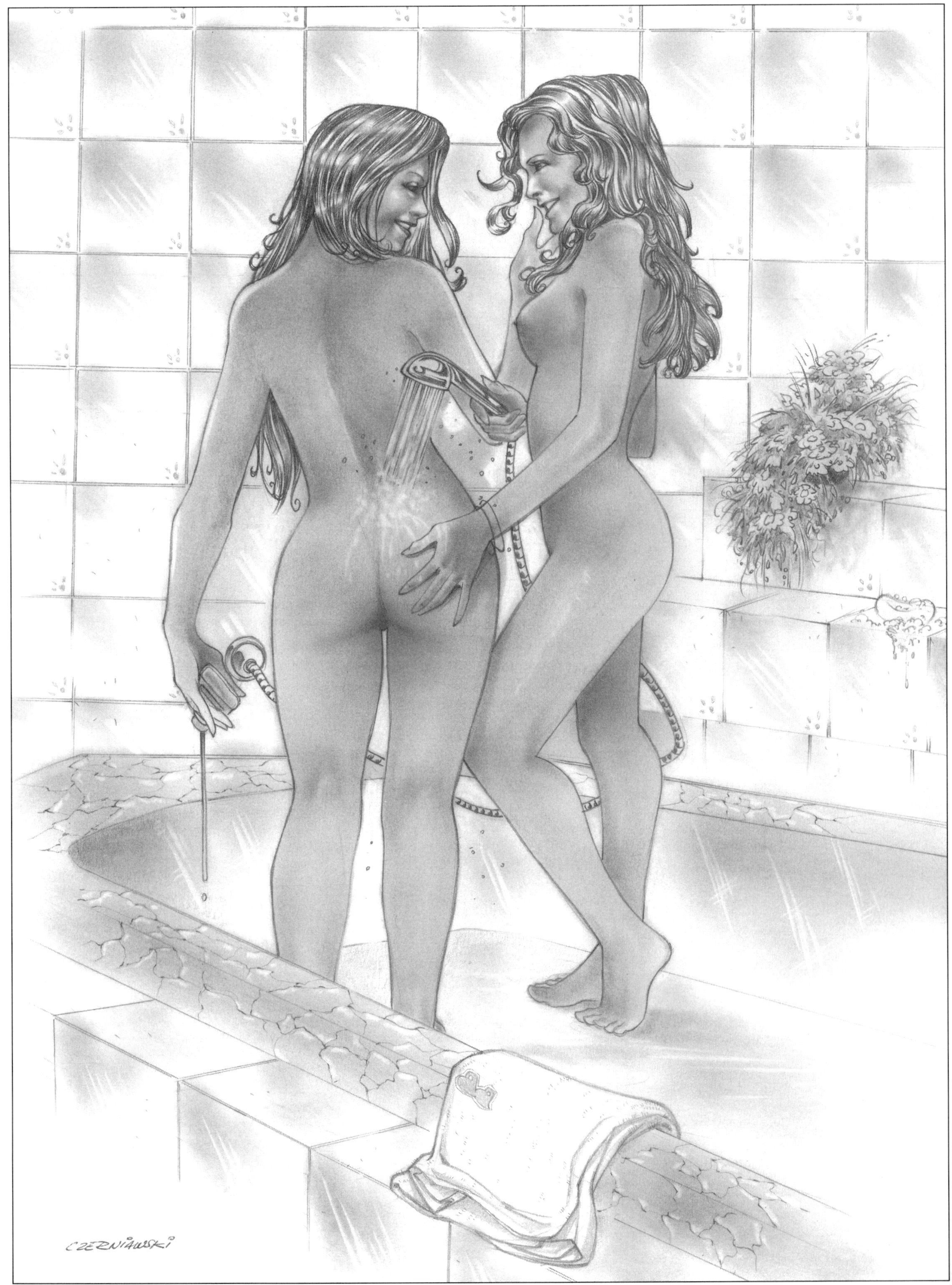

J.L. Czerniawski

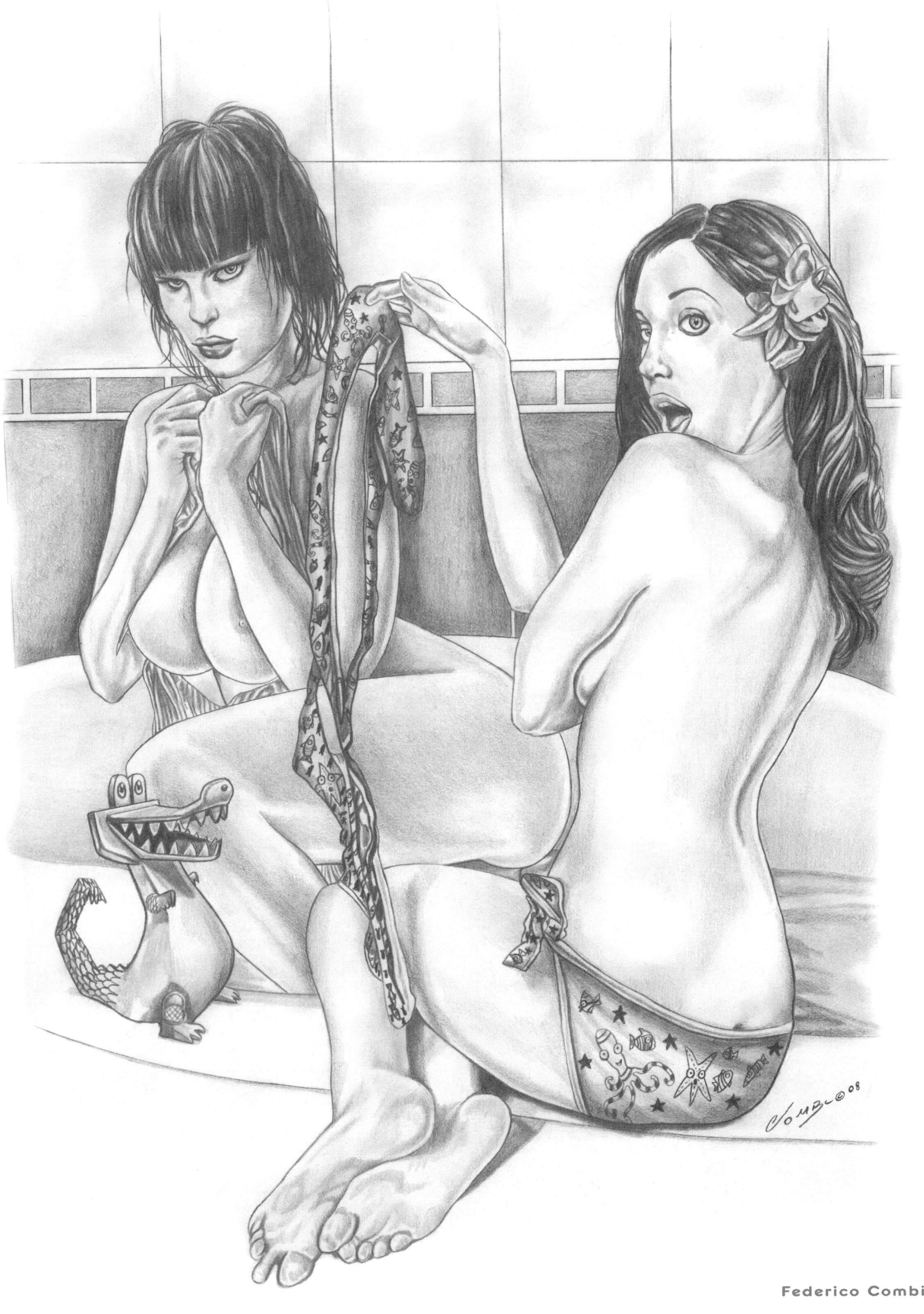

Federico Combi

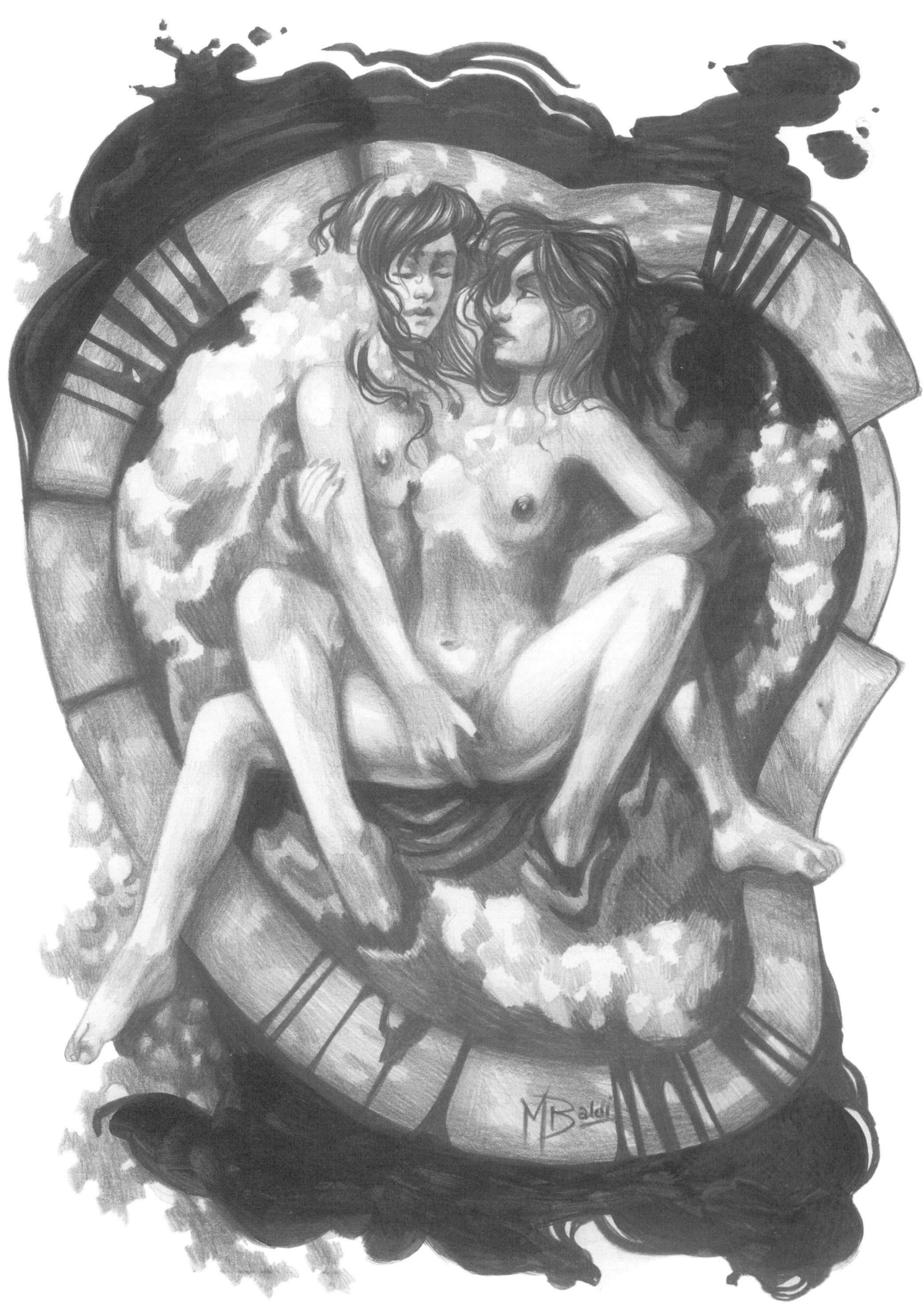

Marco Baldi

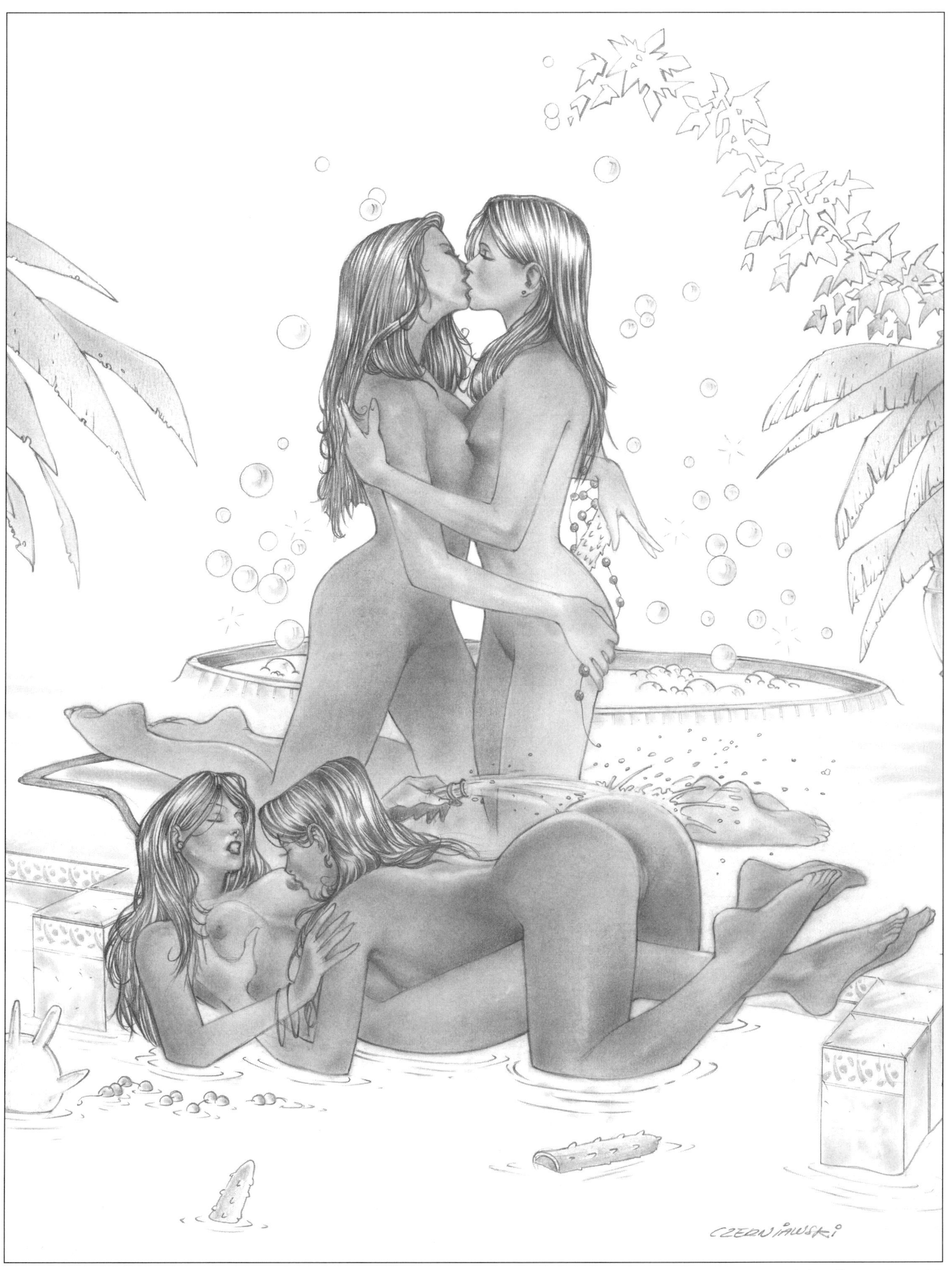

J.L. Czerniawski

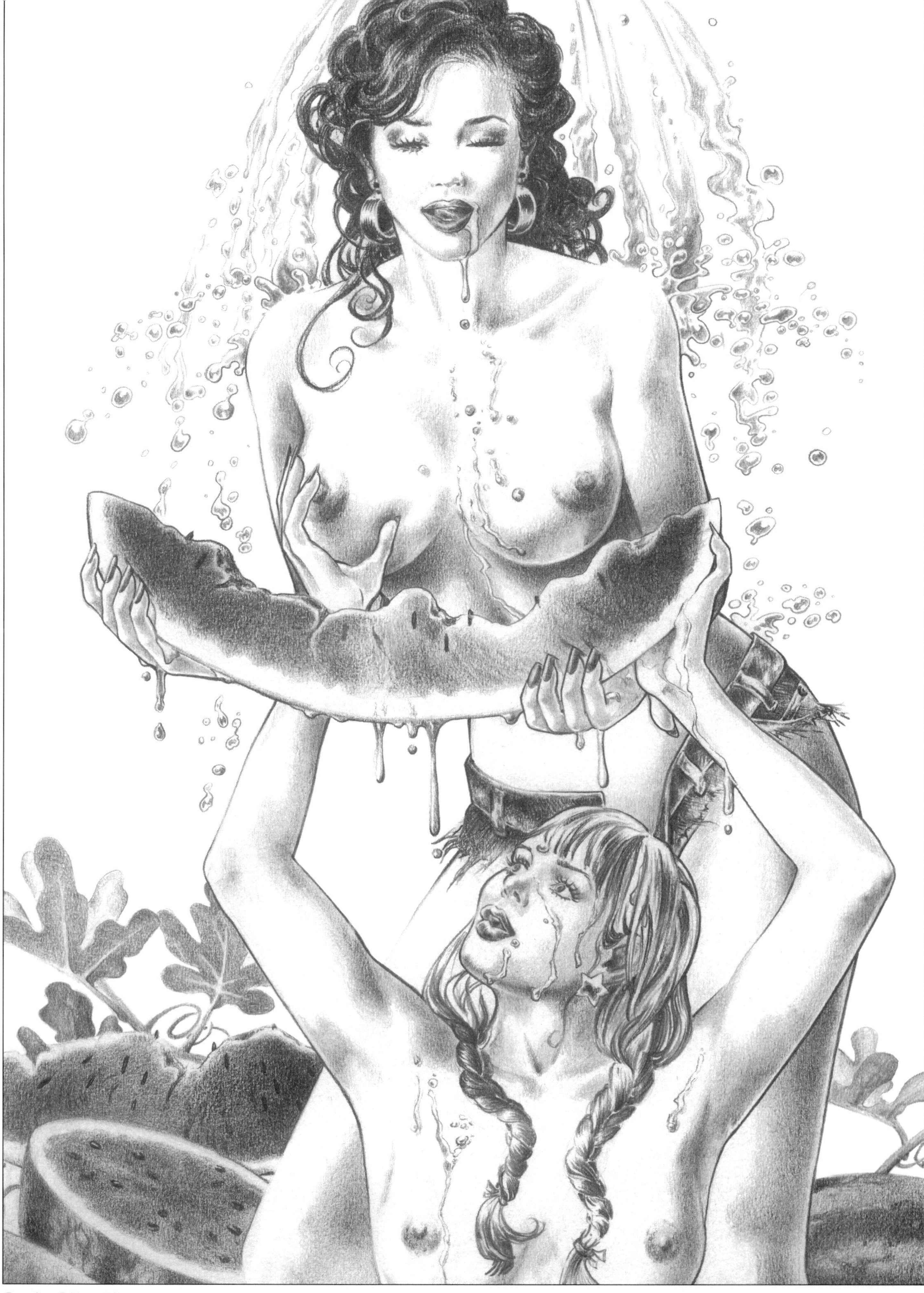

Perla Pilucki

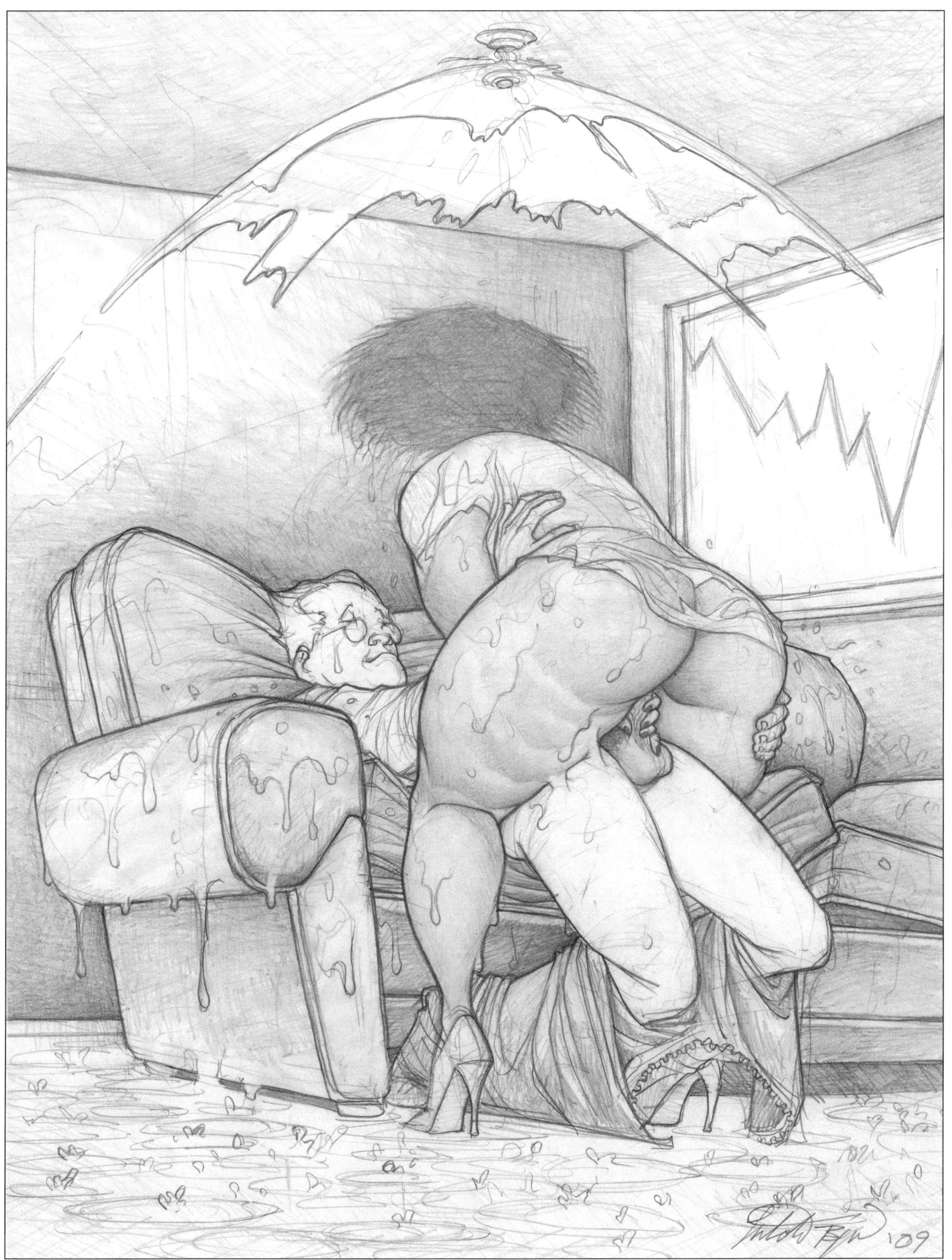

Mitch Byrd

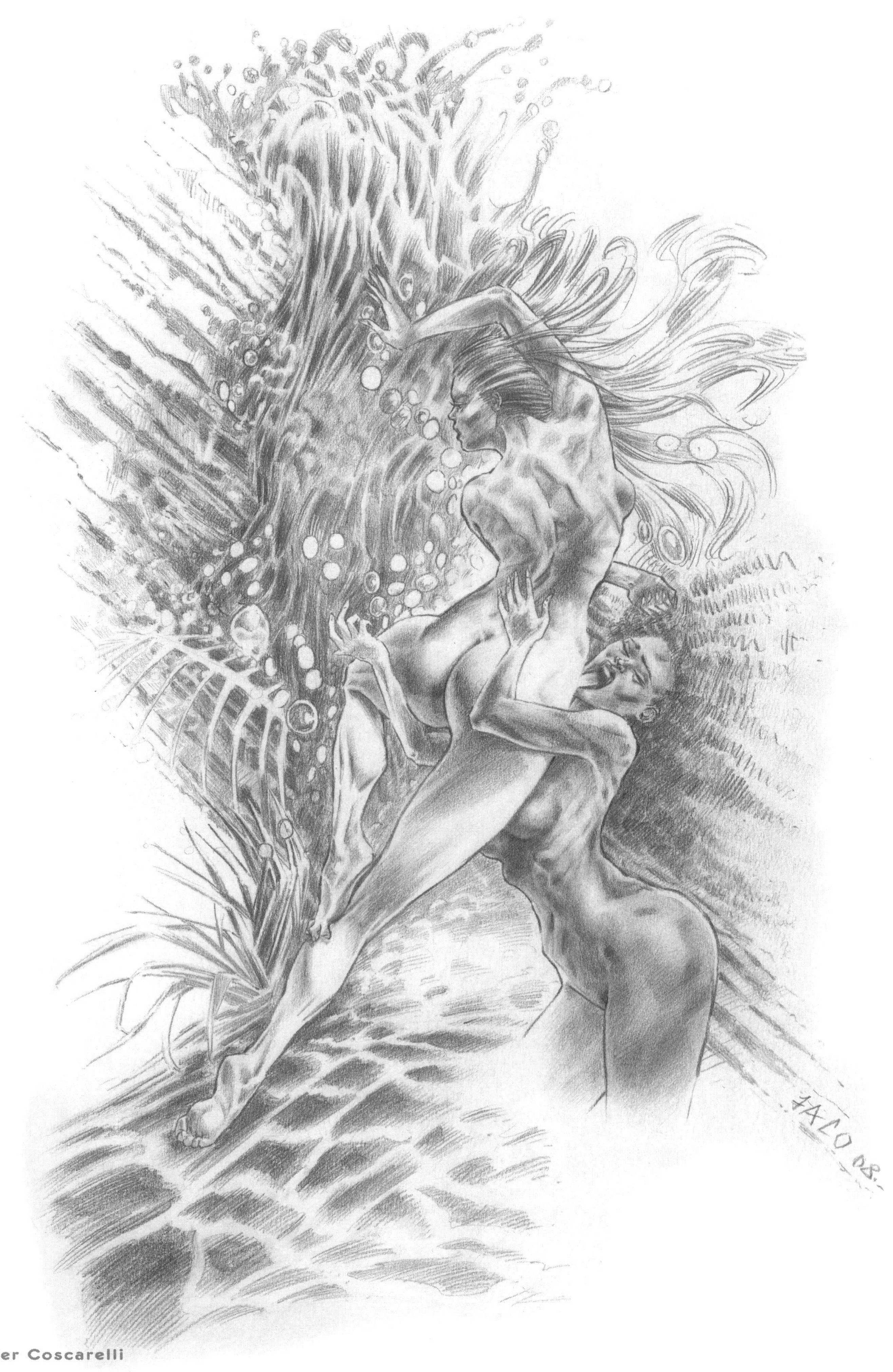

Javier Coscarelli

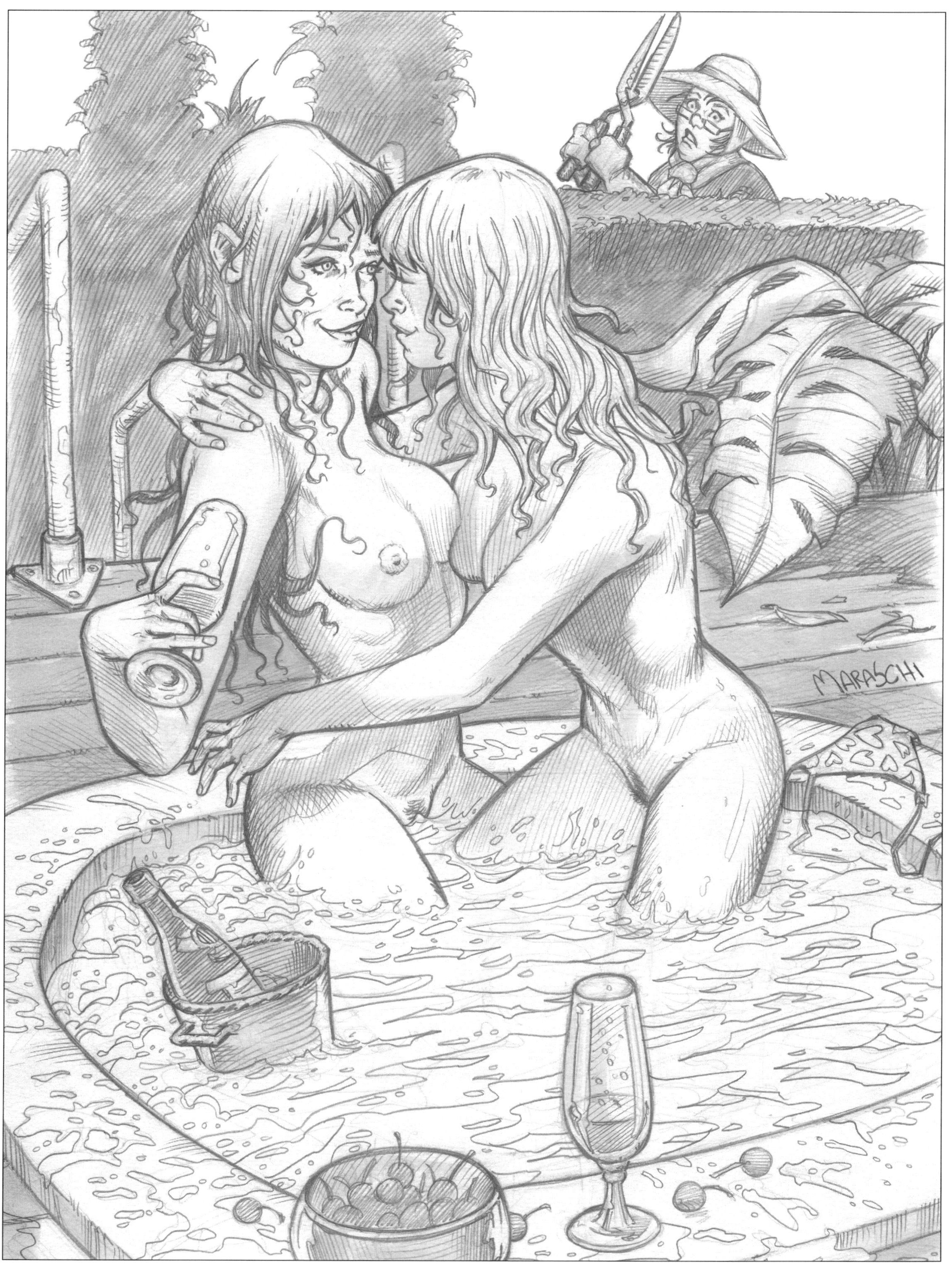

Anibal Maraschi

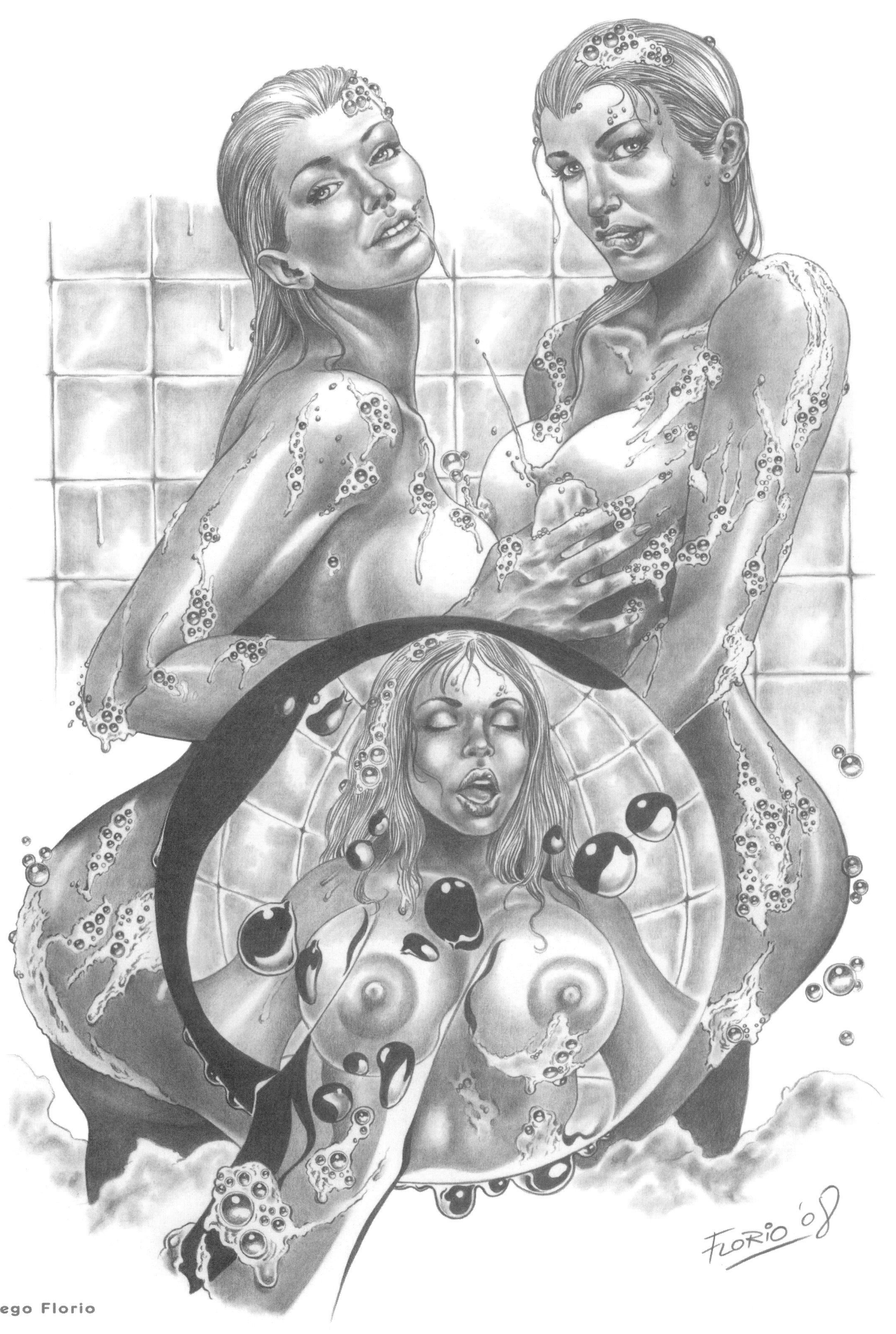

Diego Florio

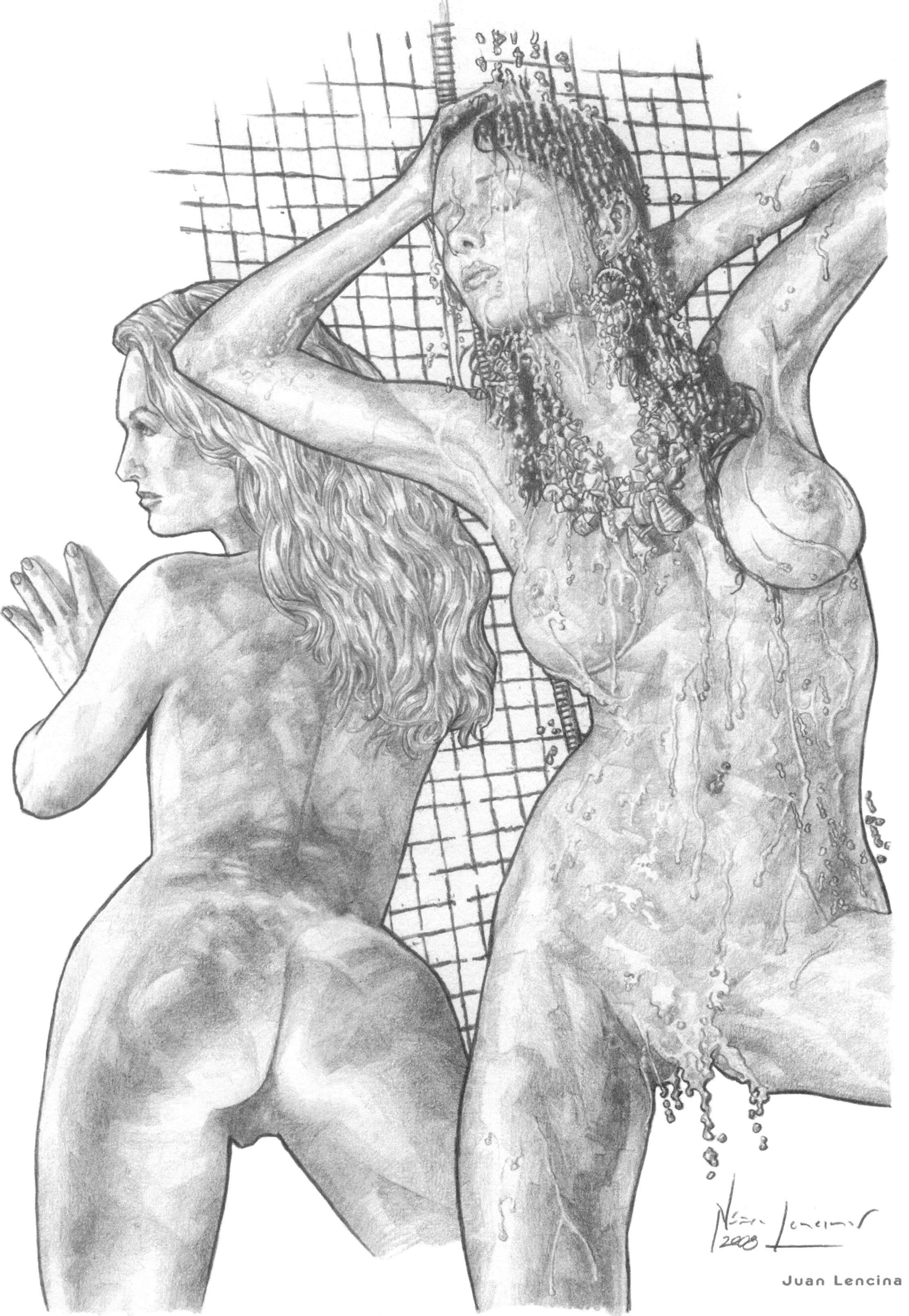

Juan Lencina

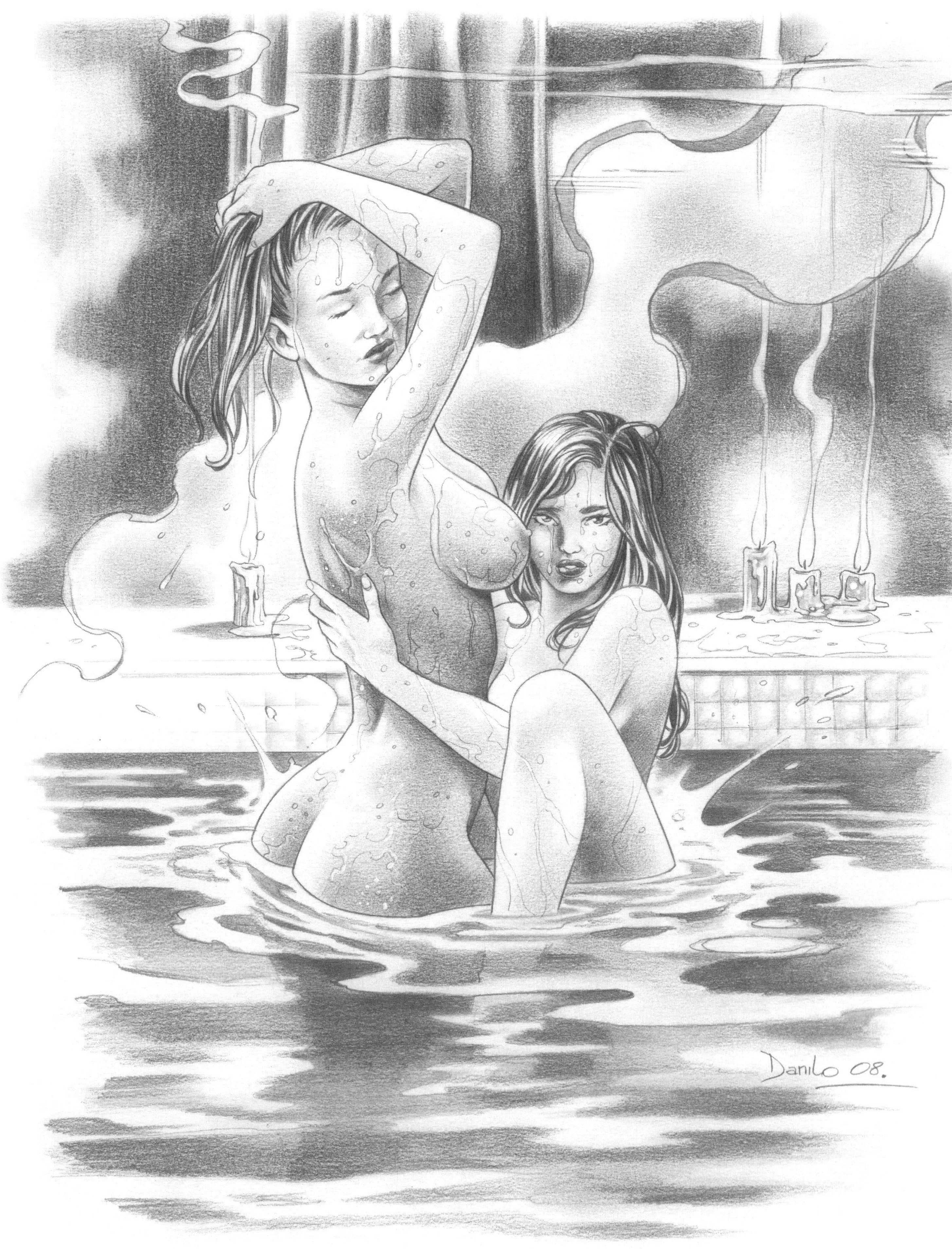

Danilo Guida

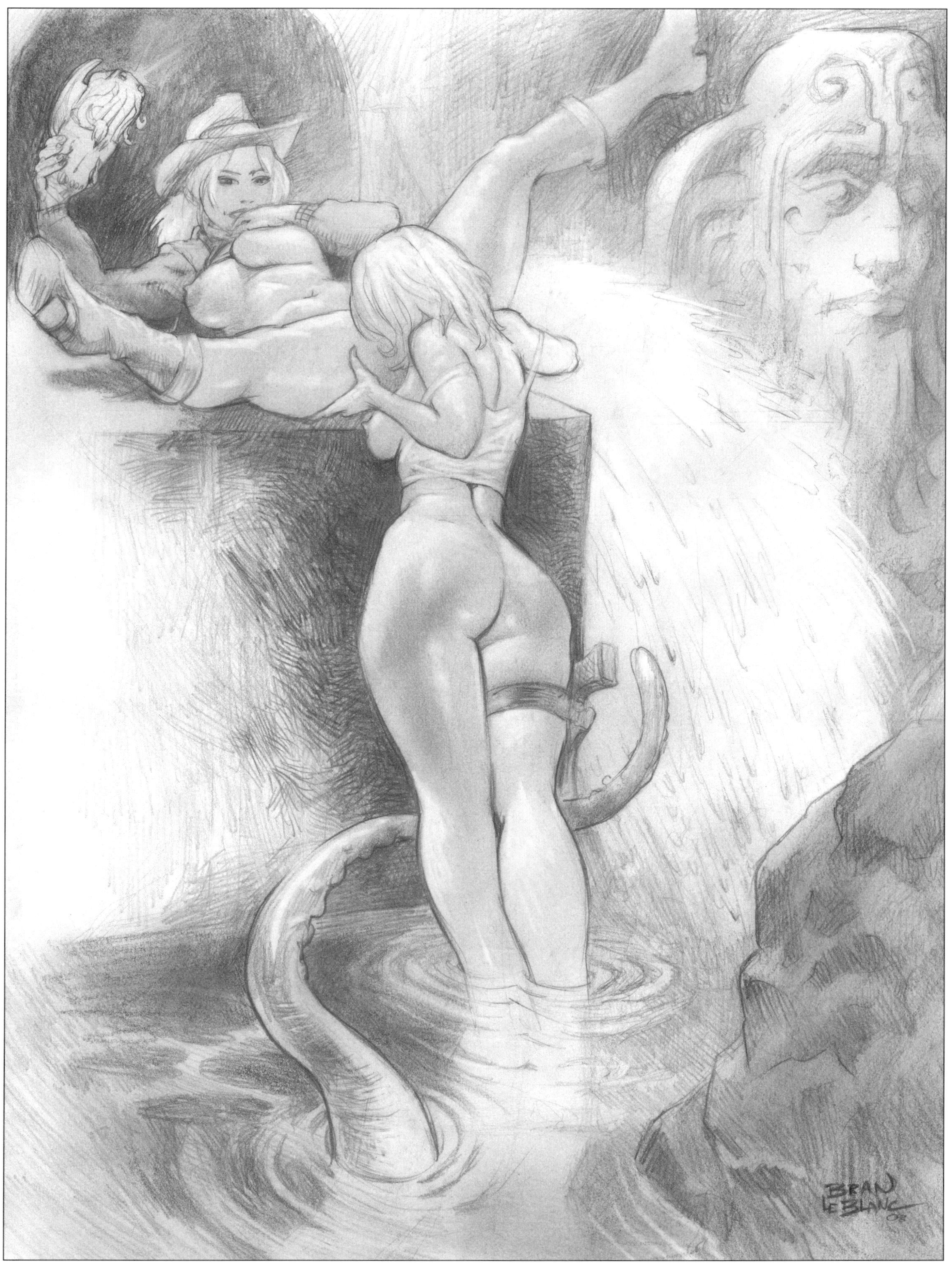

Brian LeBlanc

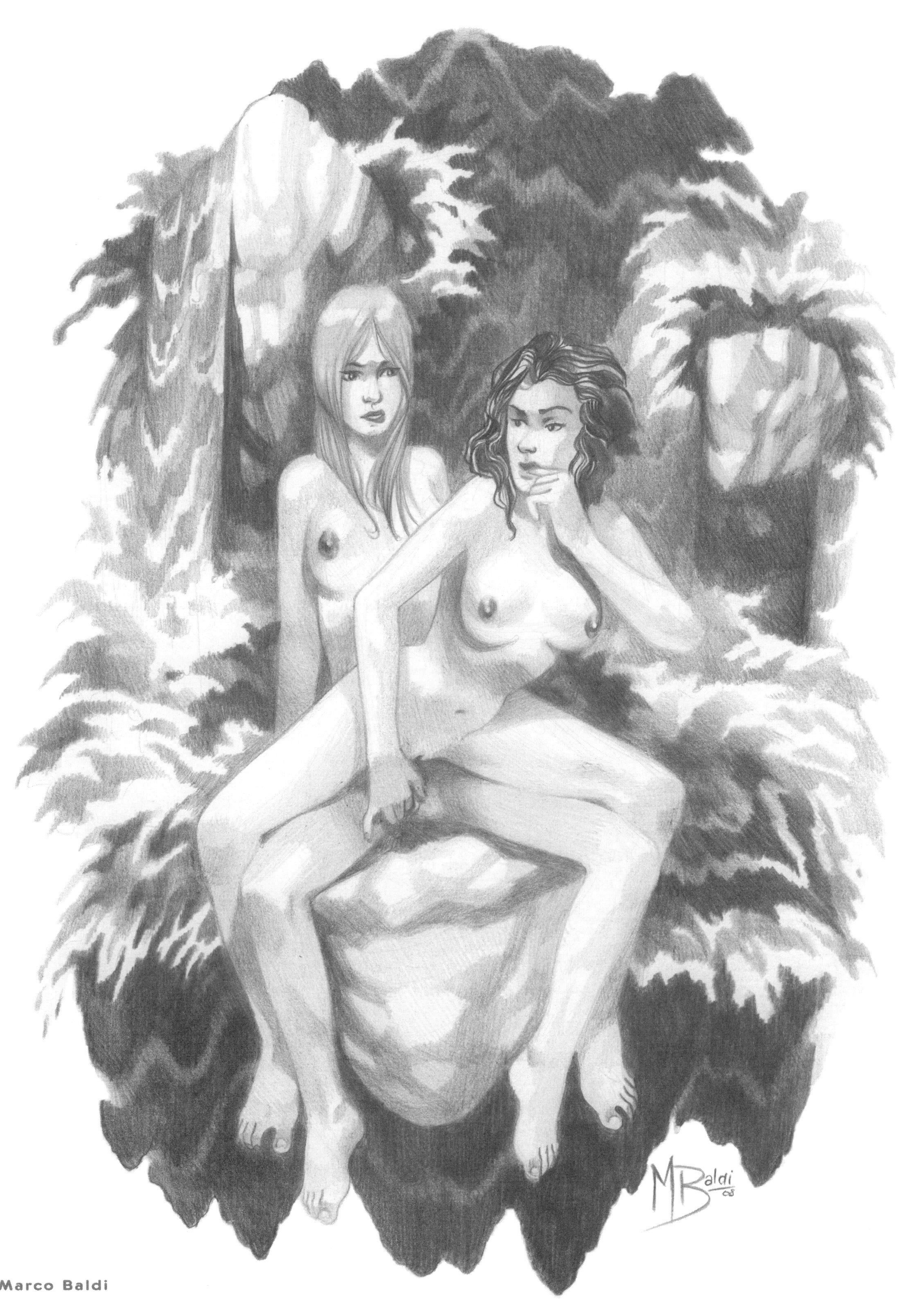

Marco Baldi

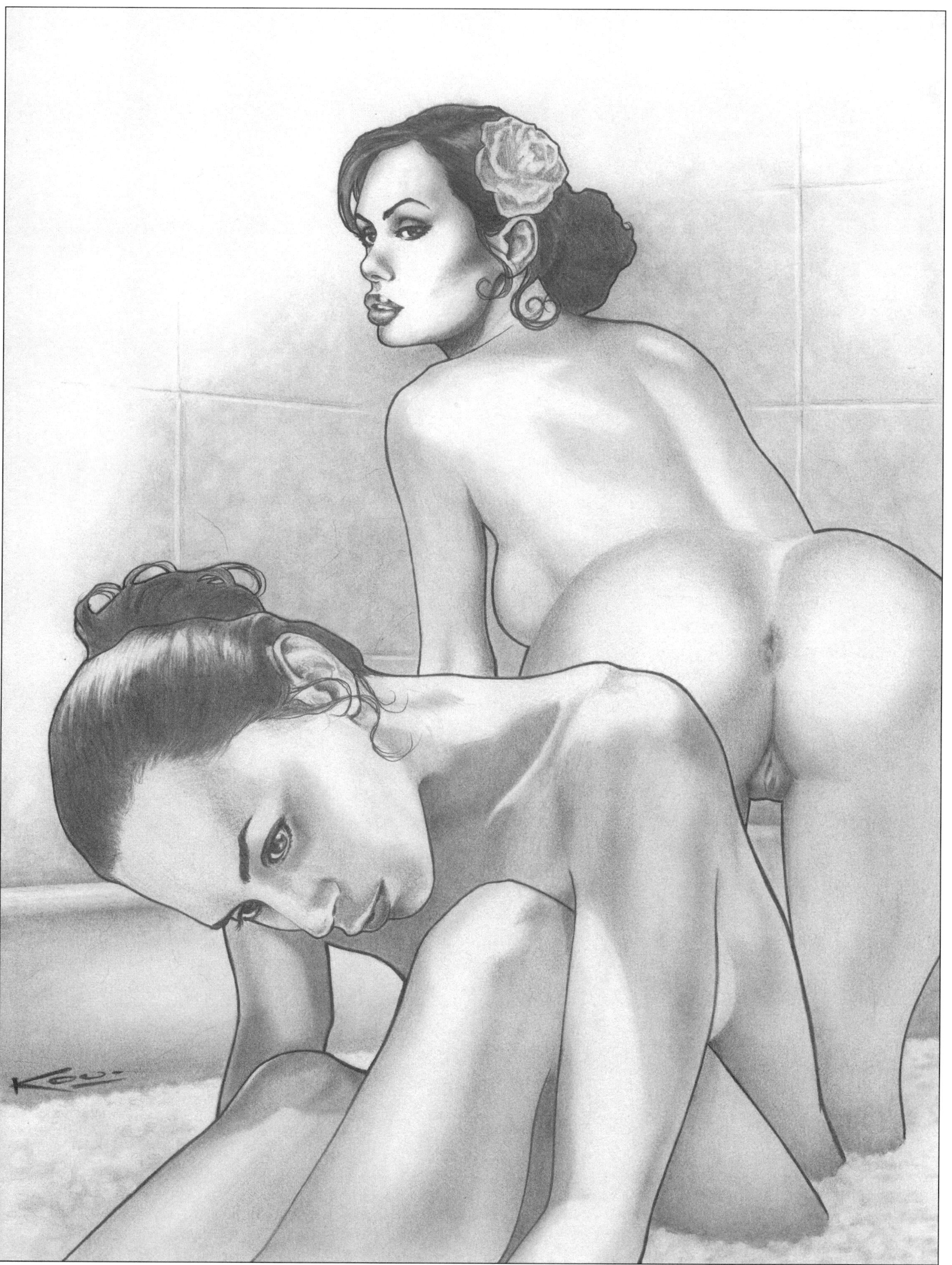

Pablo Kousovitis

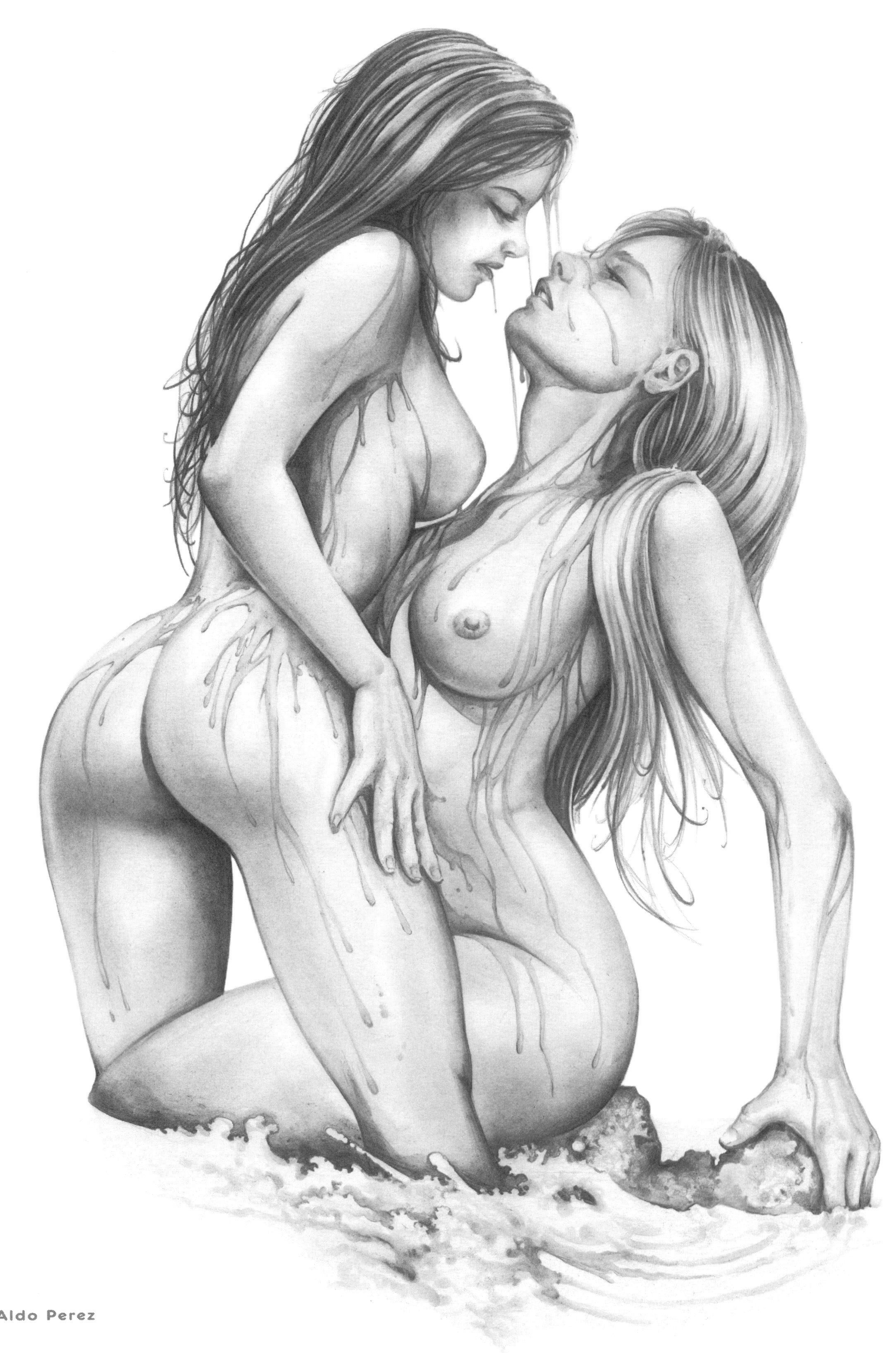

Aldo Perez

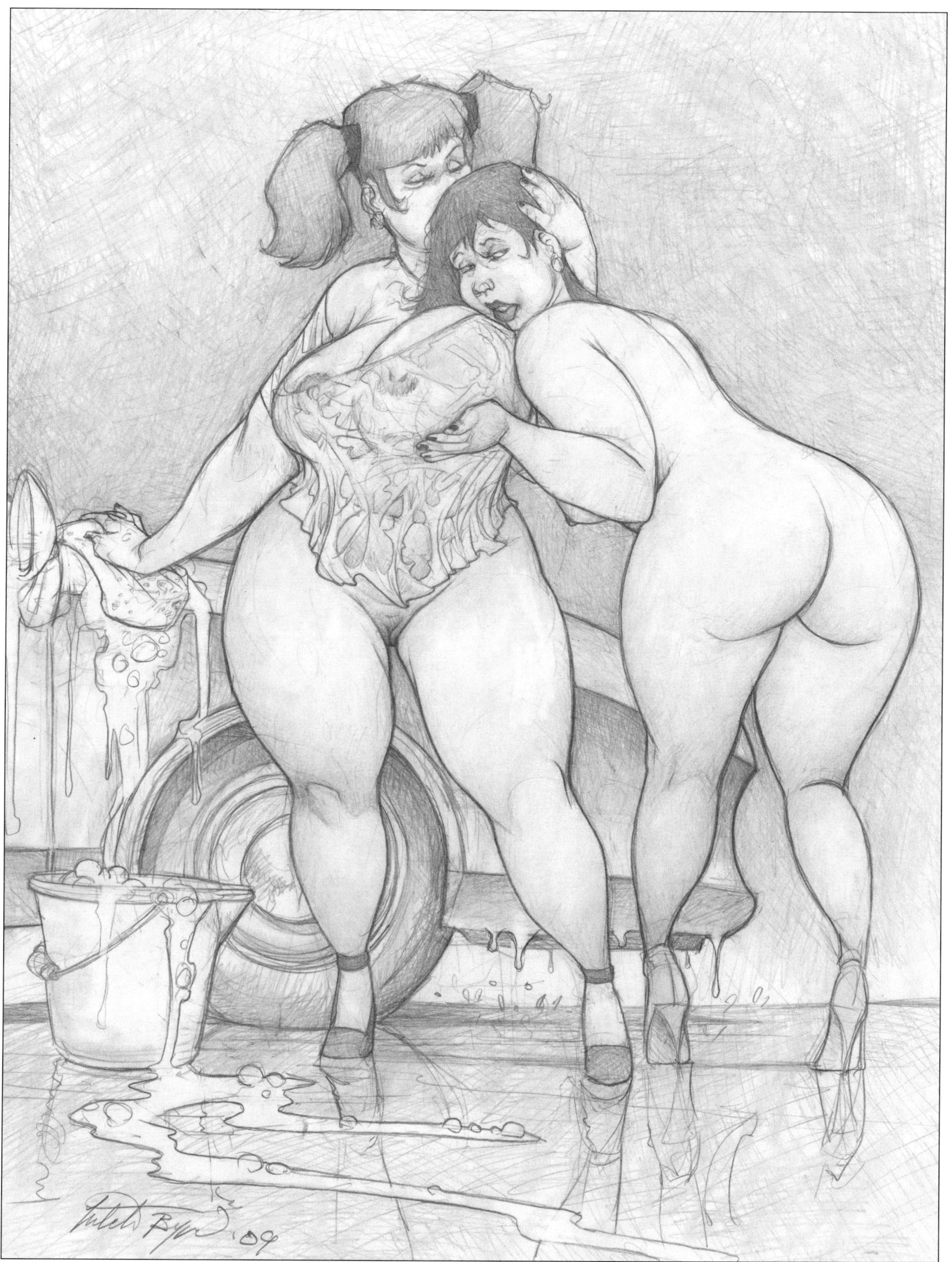

Mitch Byrd

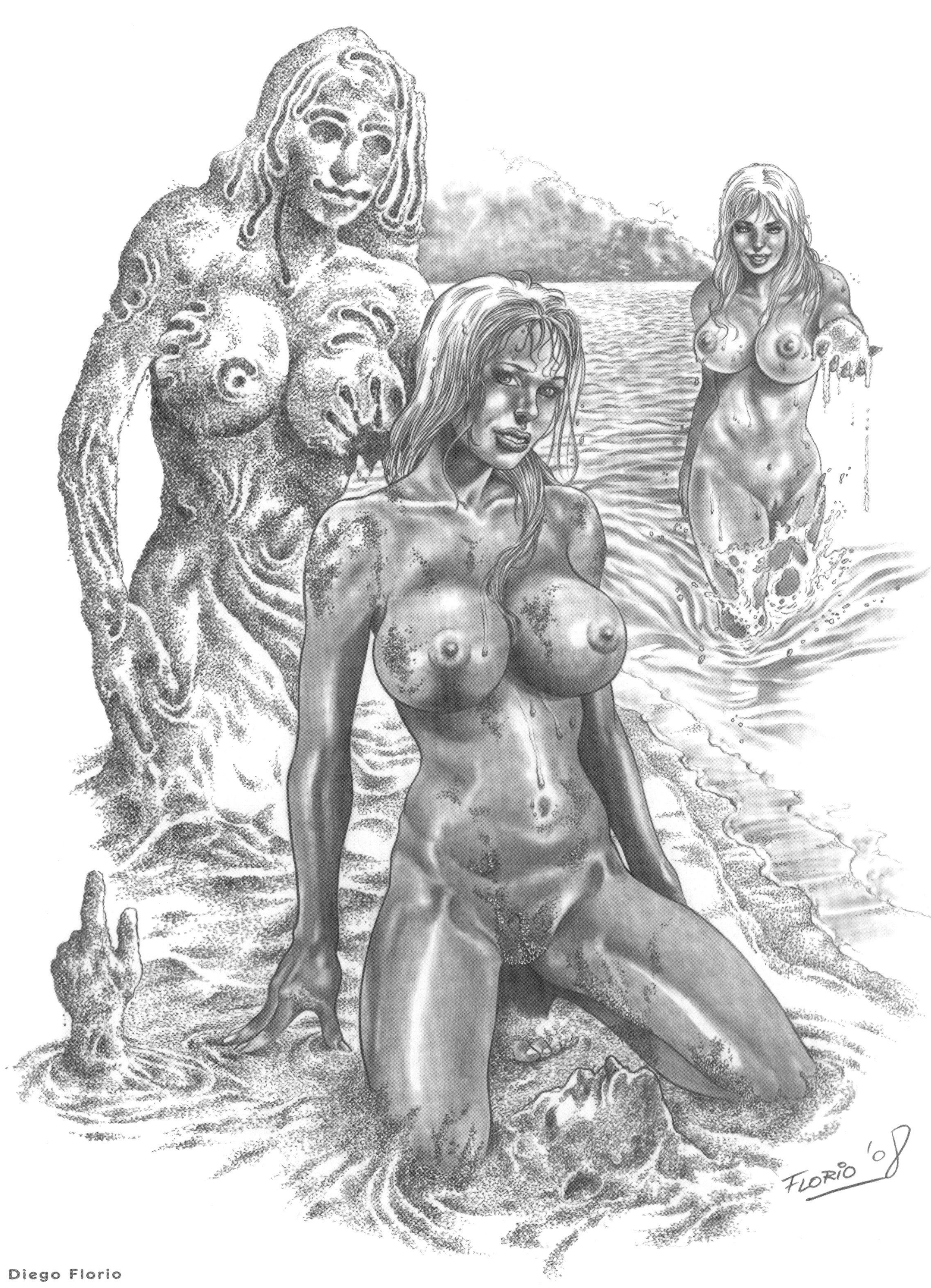

Diego Florio

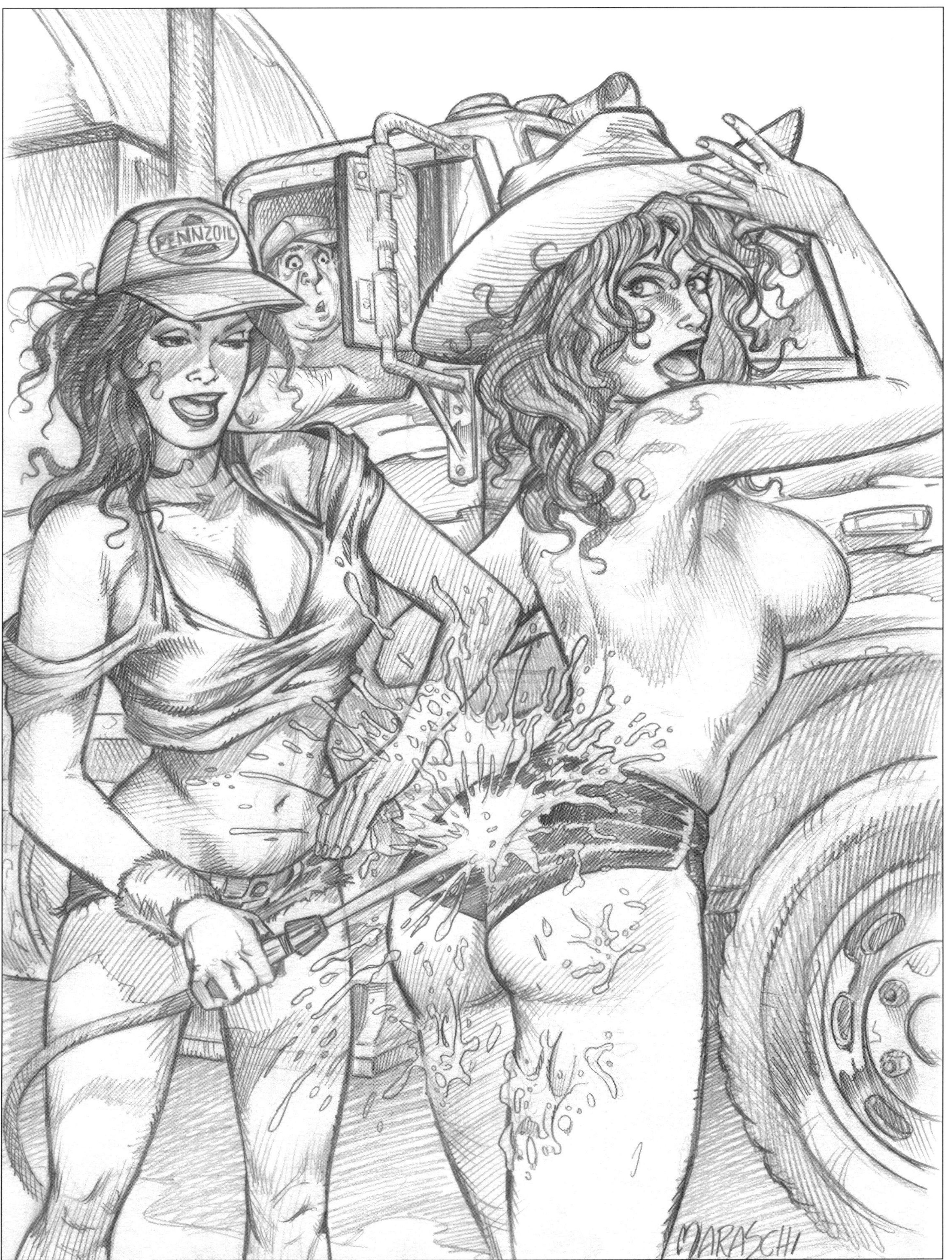

Anibal Maraschi

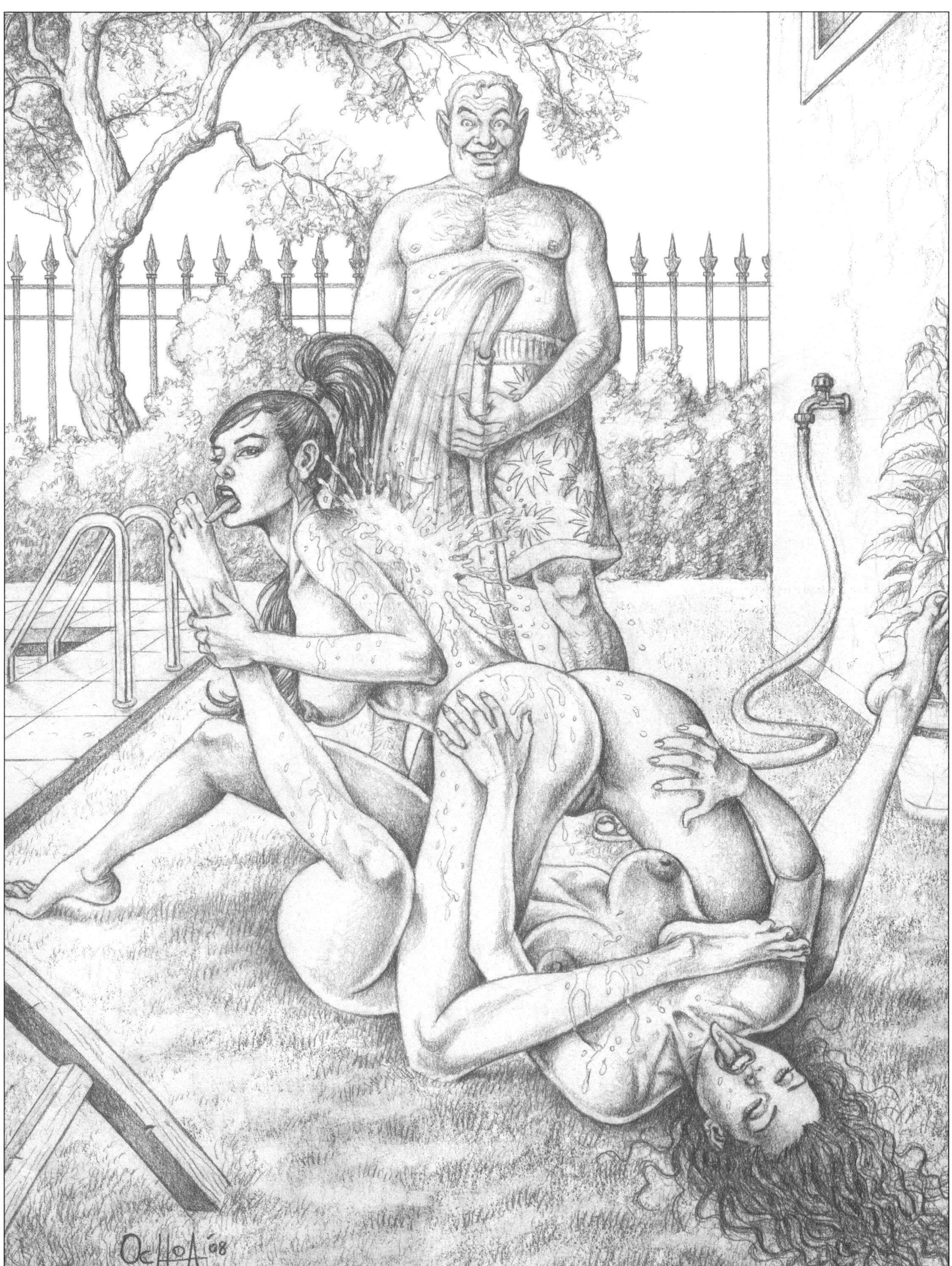

Percy Ochoa

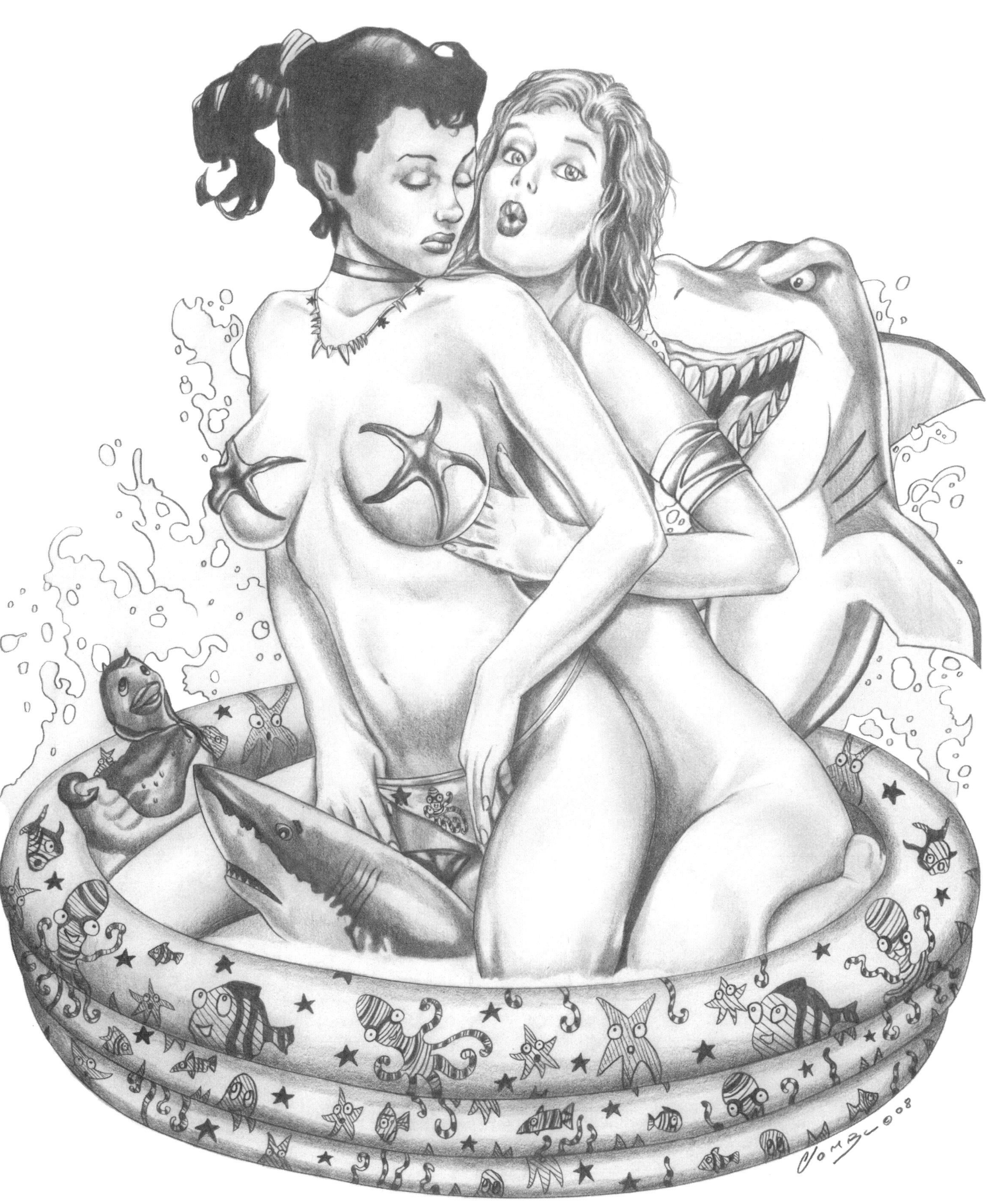

Federico Combi

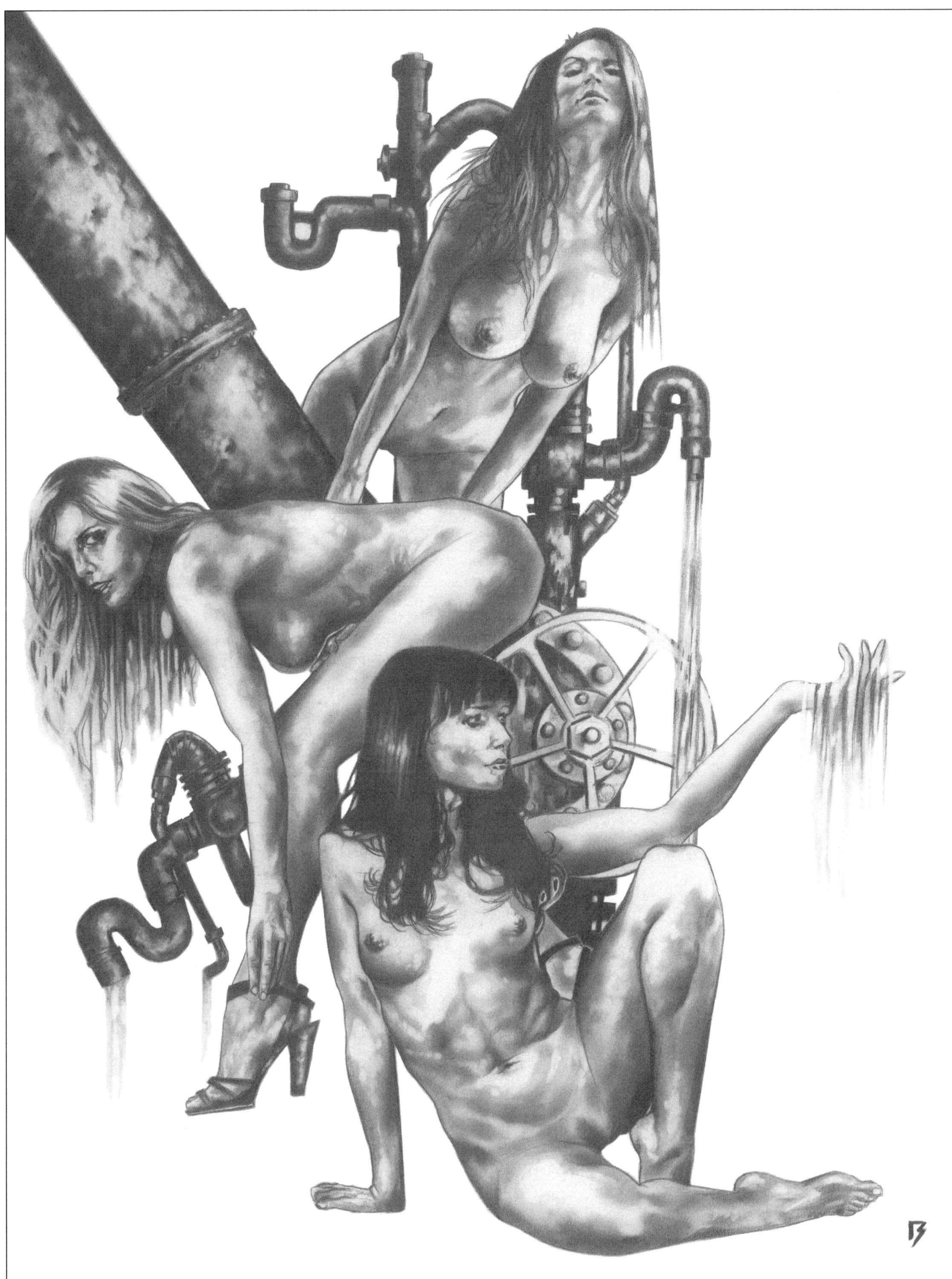

Luis Buci

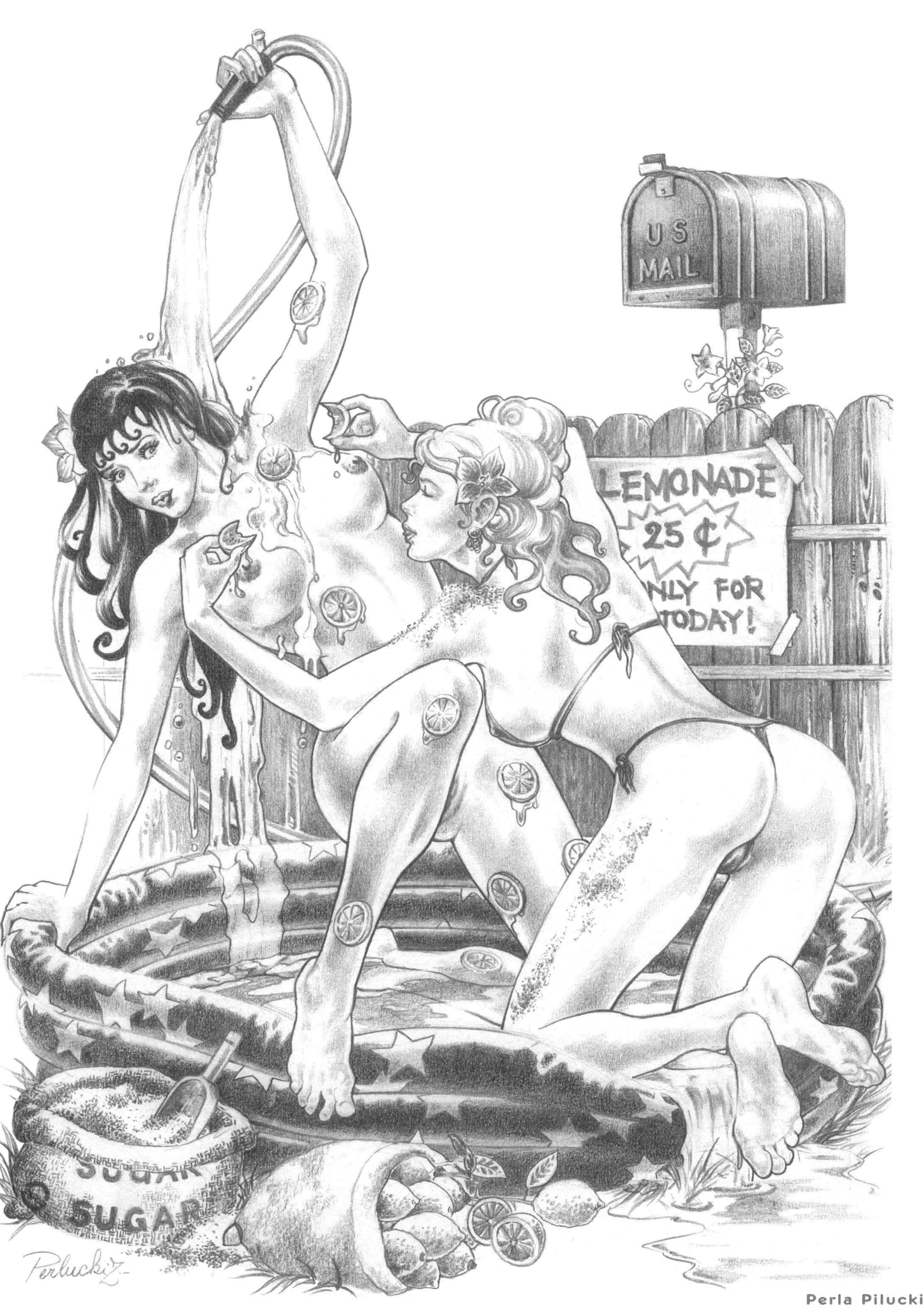

Perla Pilucki

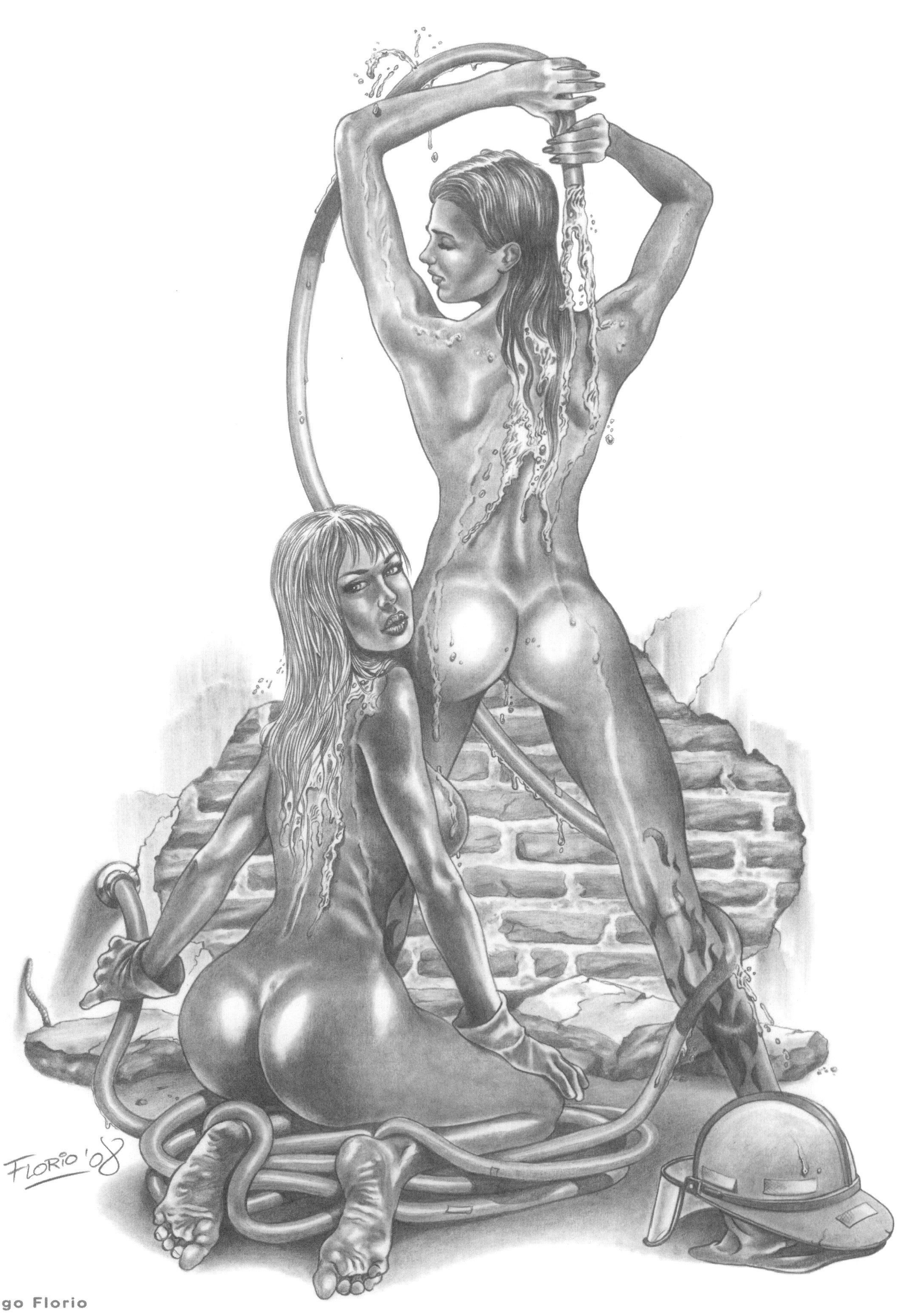

Diego Florio

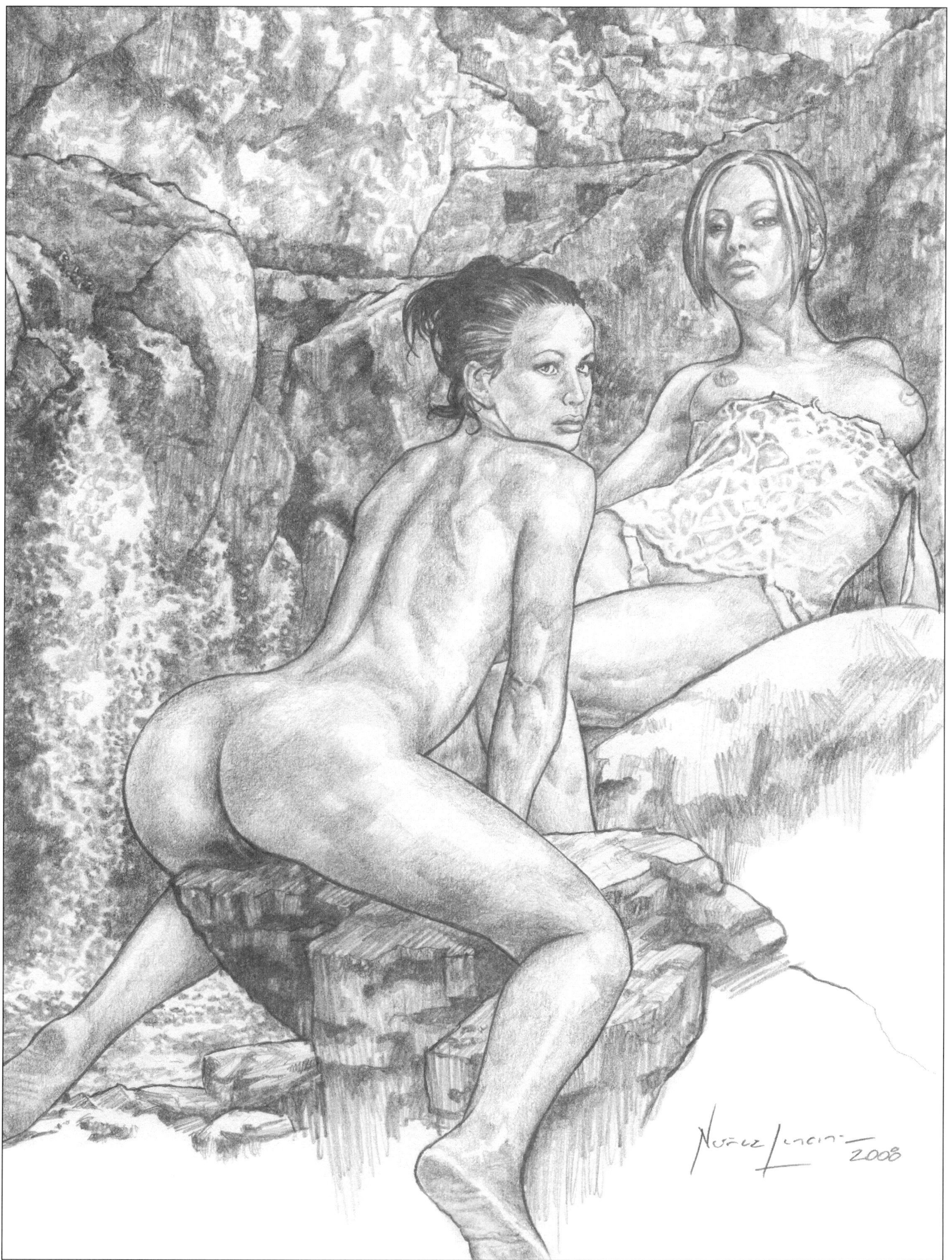

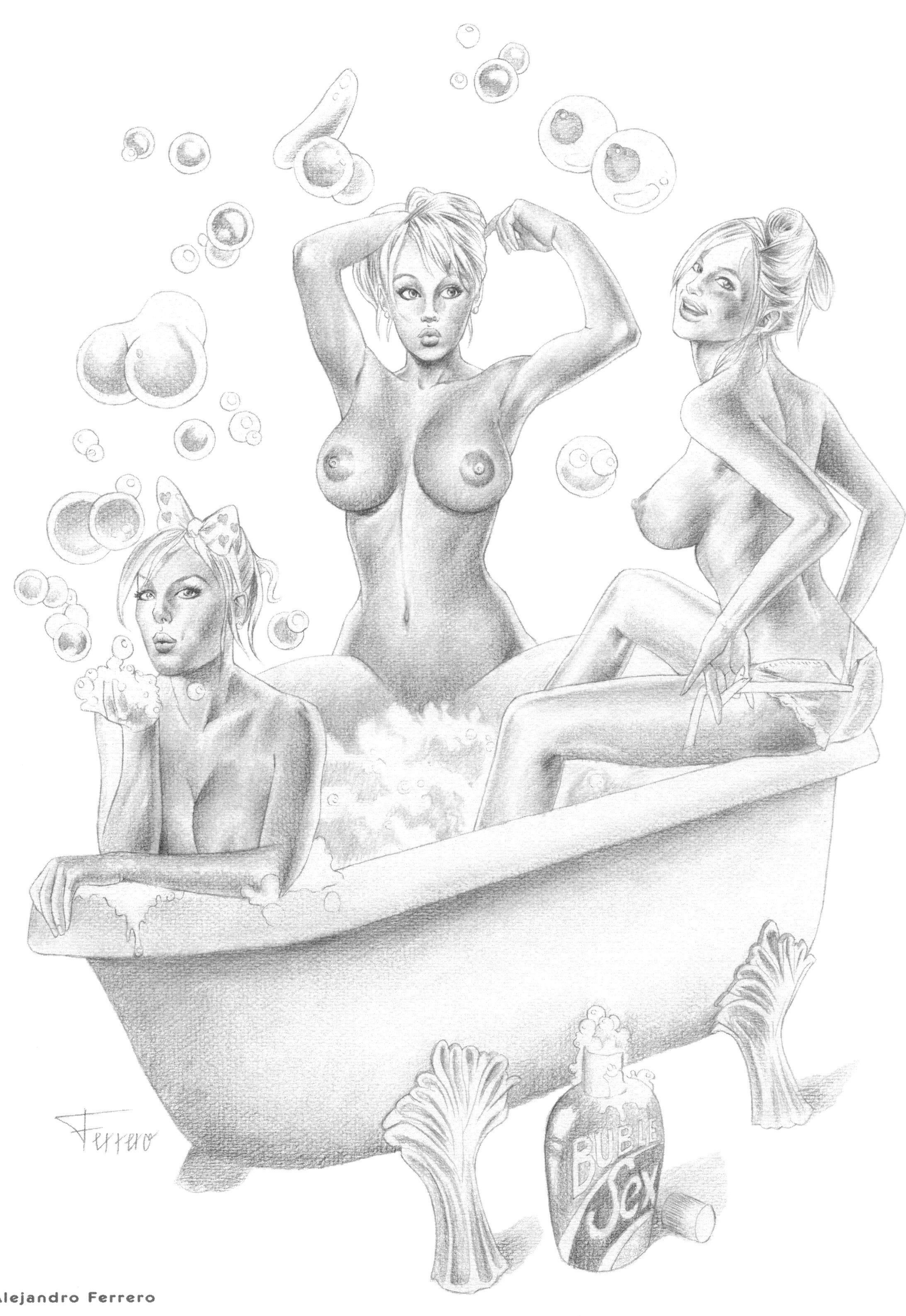

Alejandro Ferrero

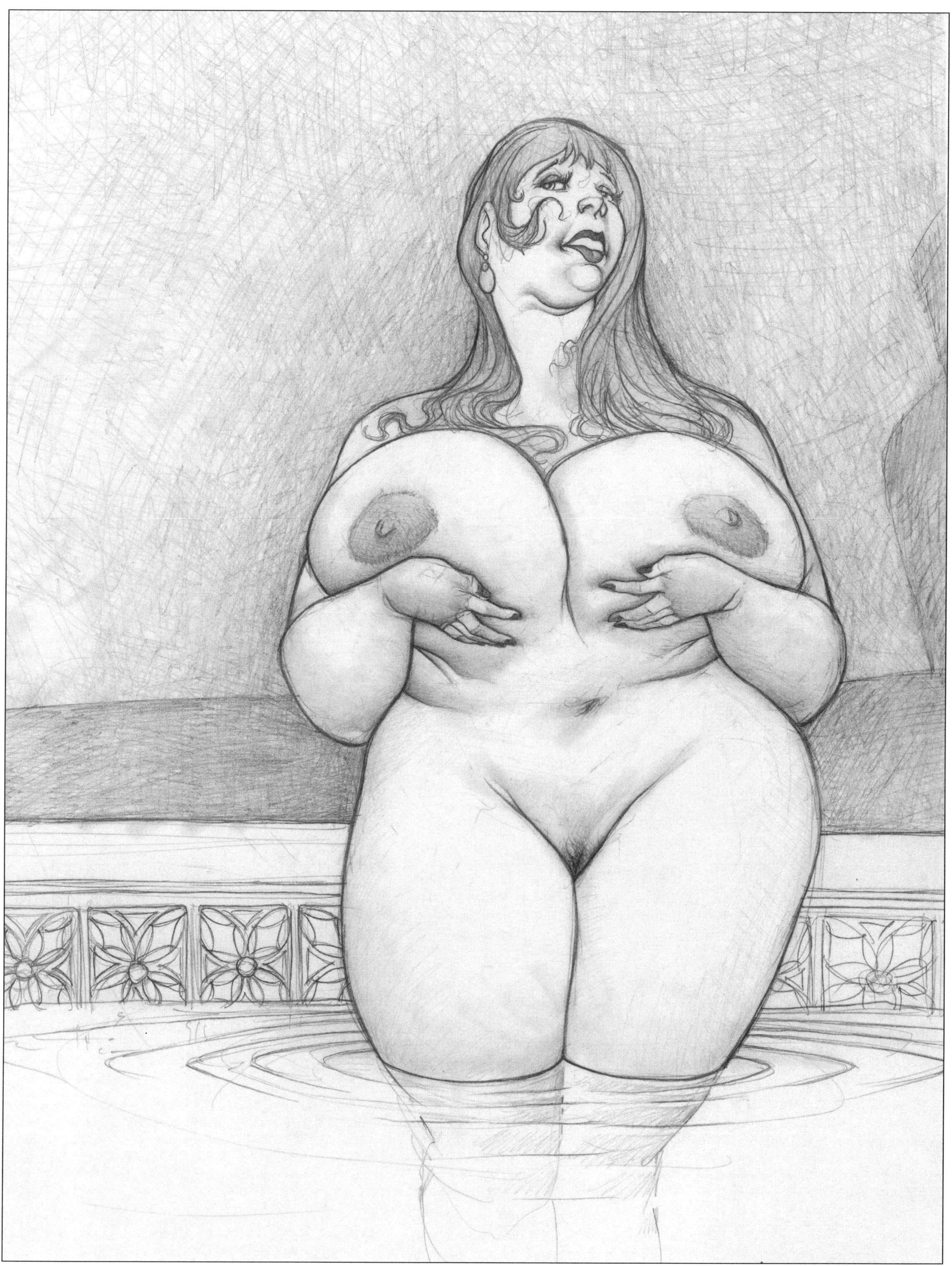

Mitch Byrd

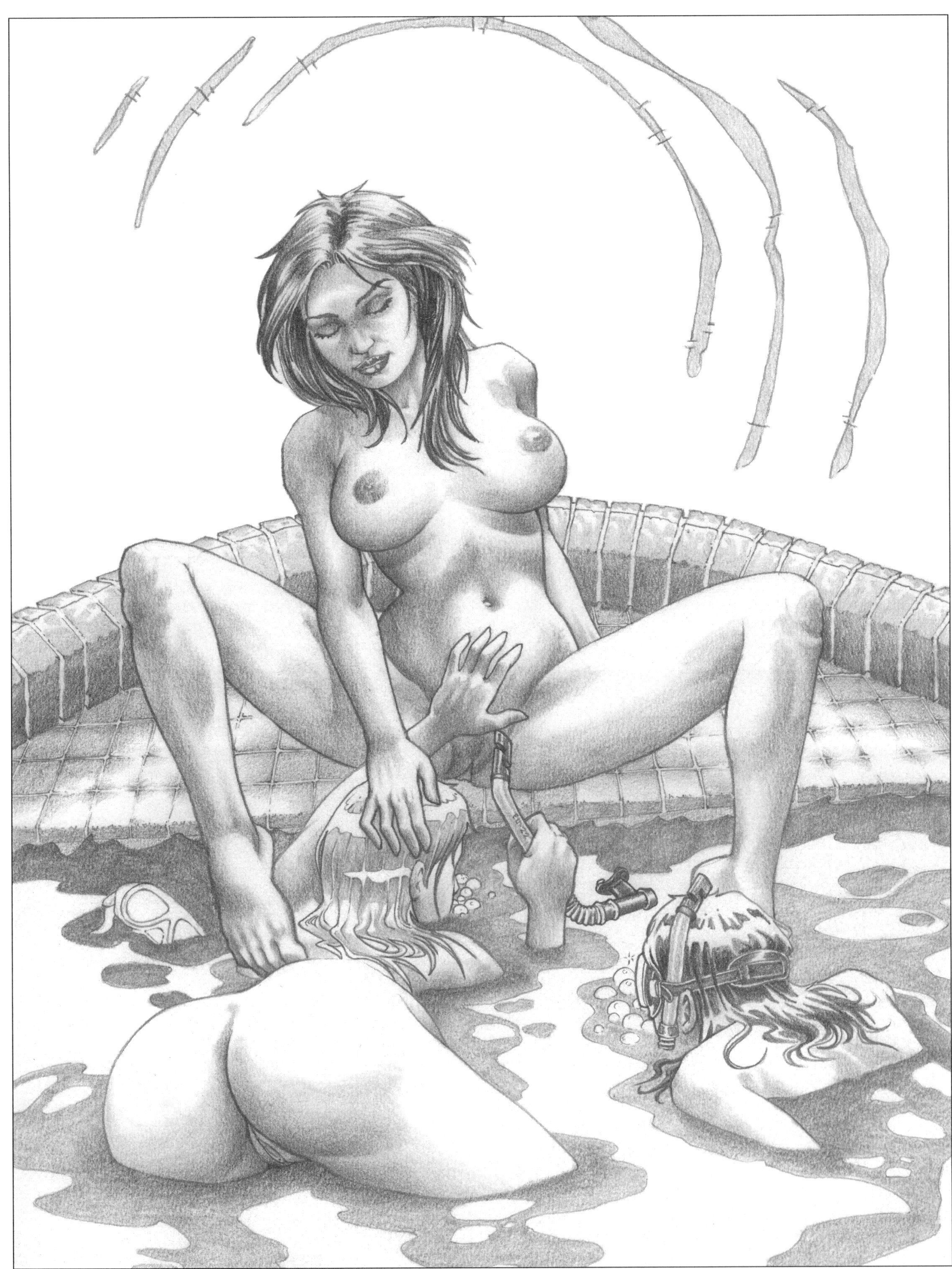

Emiliano Urdinola

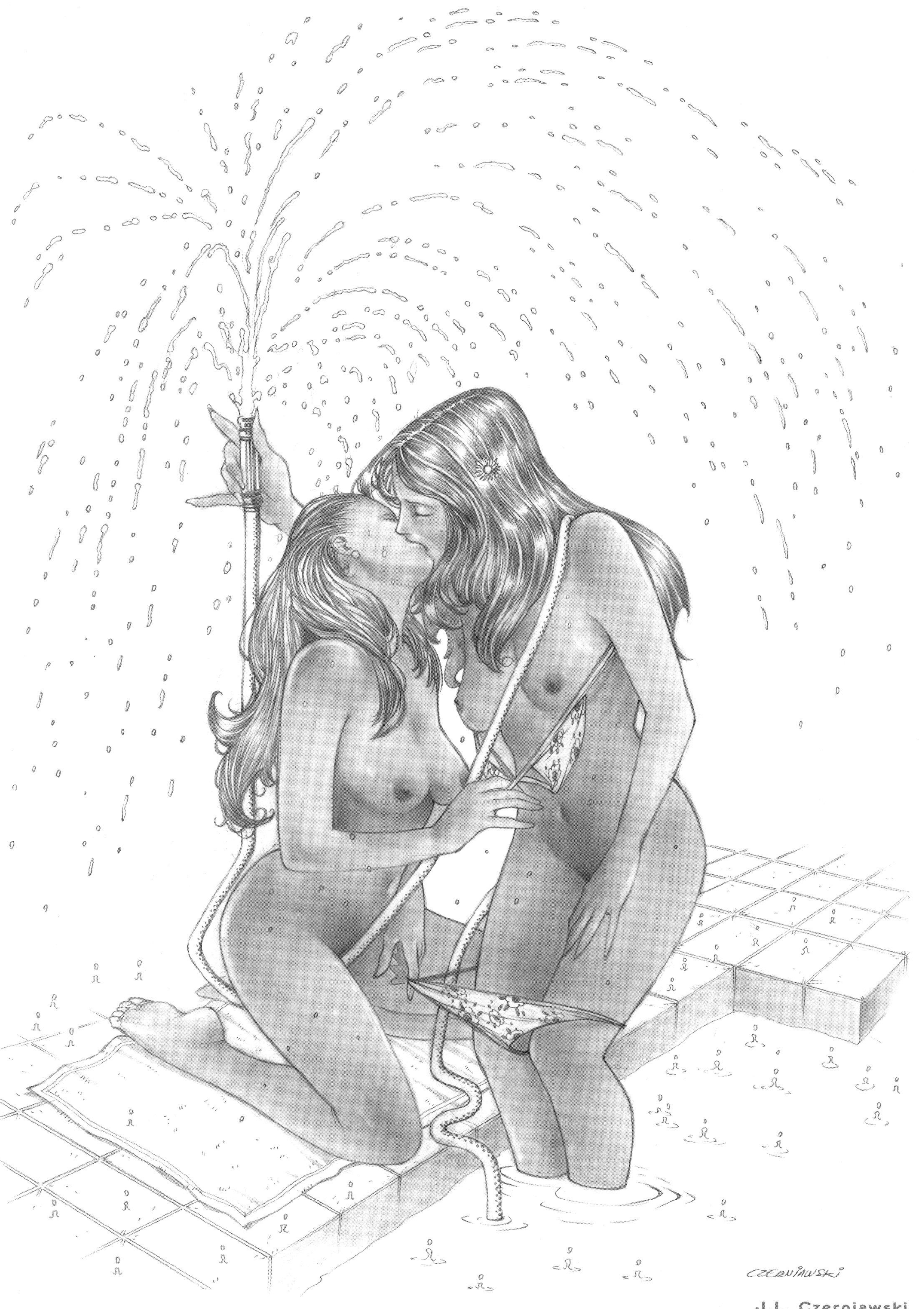

J.L. Czerniawski

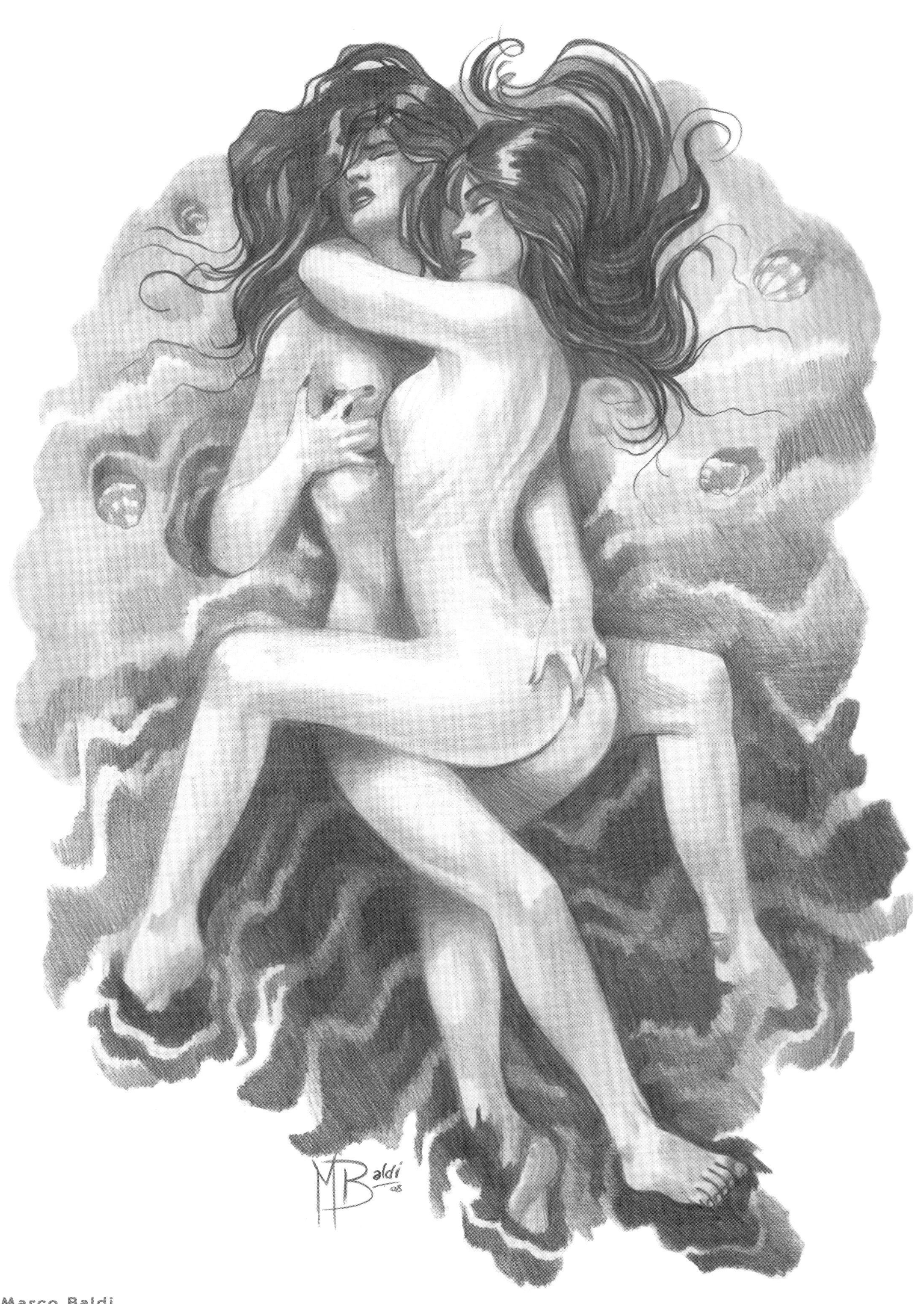

Marco Baldi

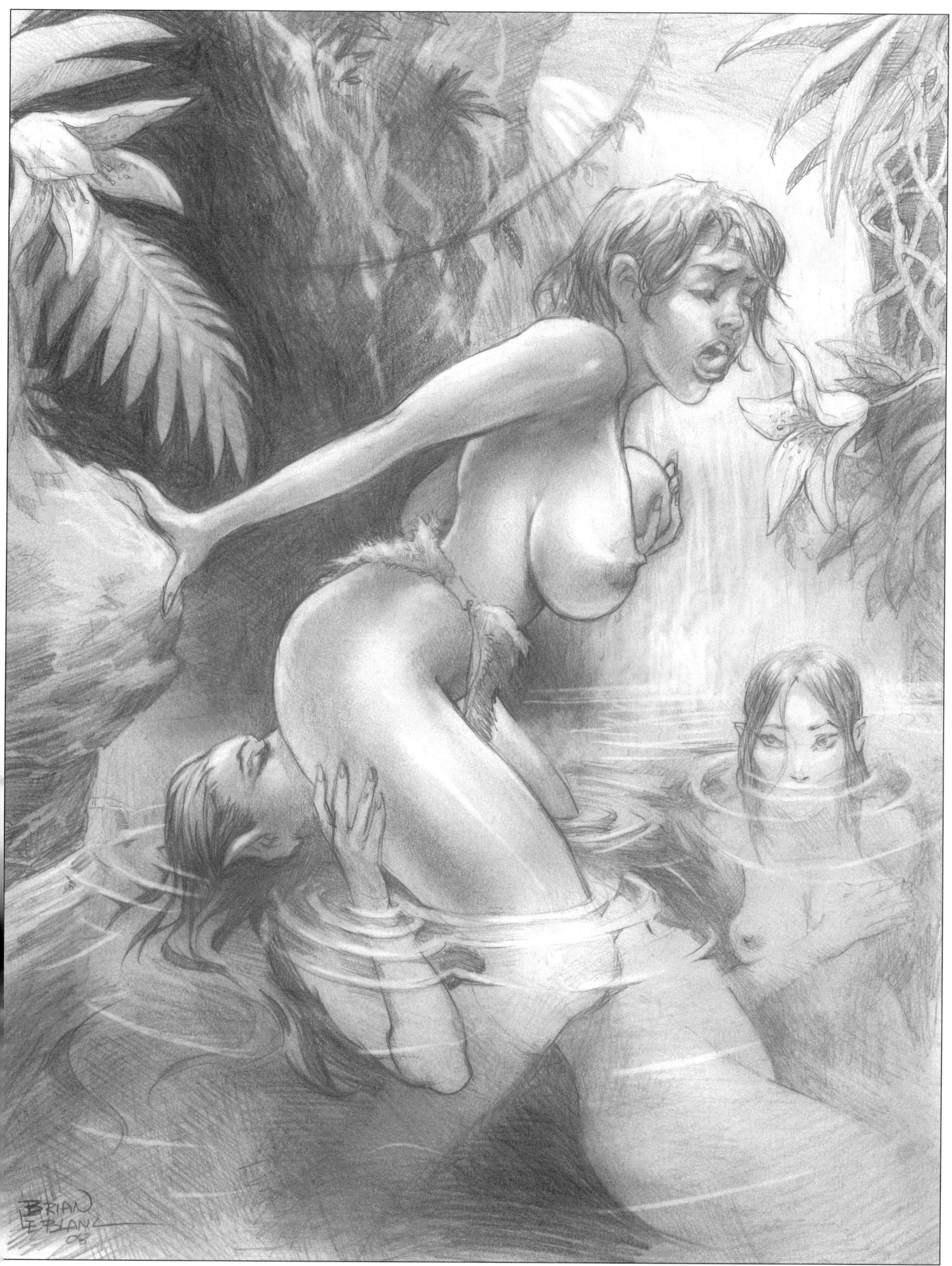

Brian LeBlanc

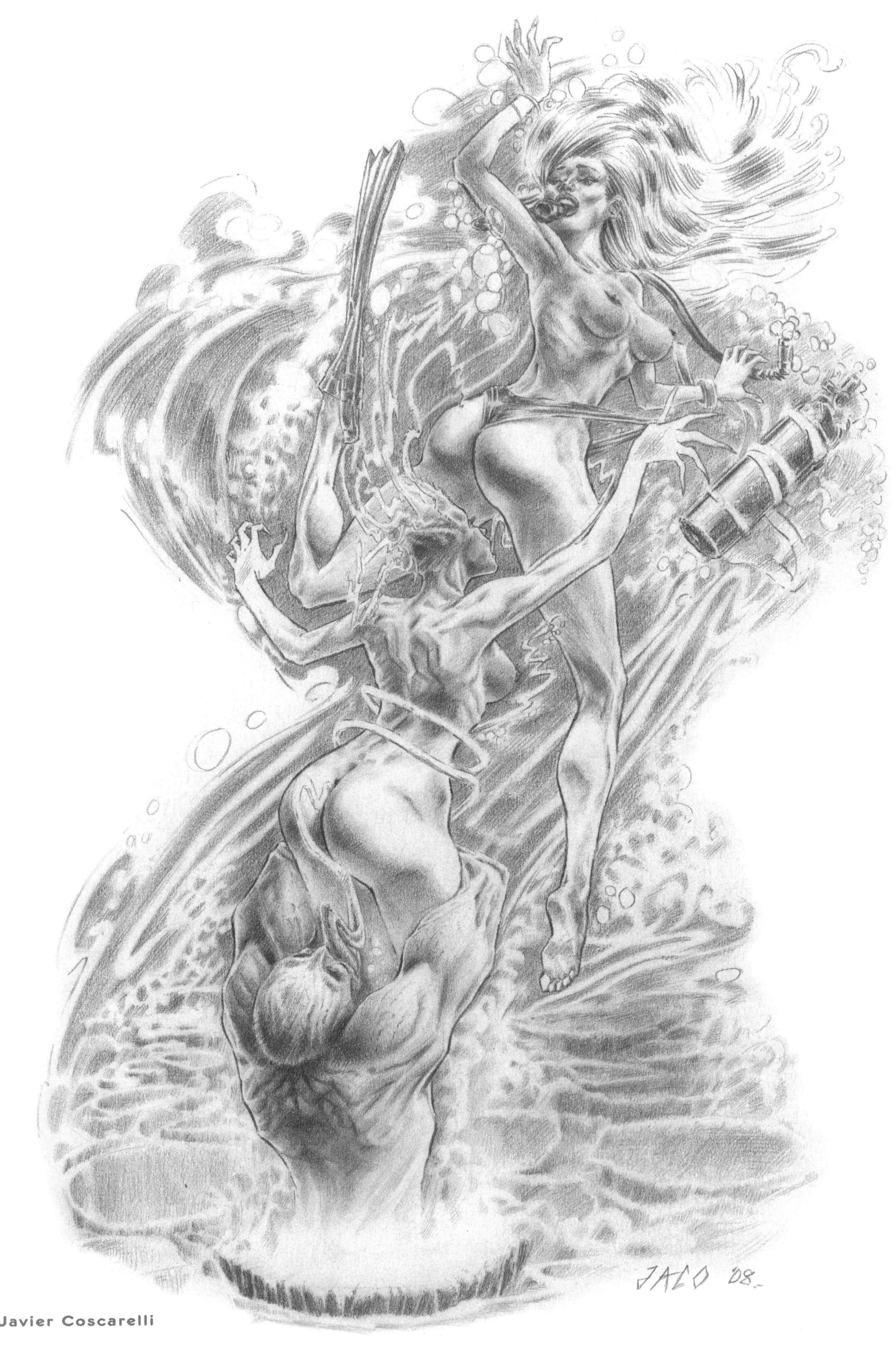

Javier Coscarelli

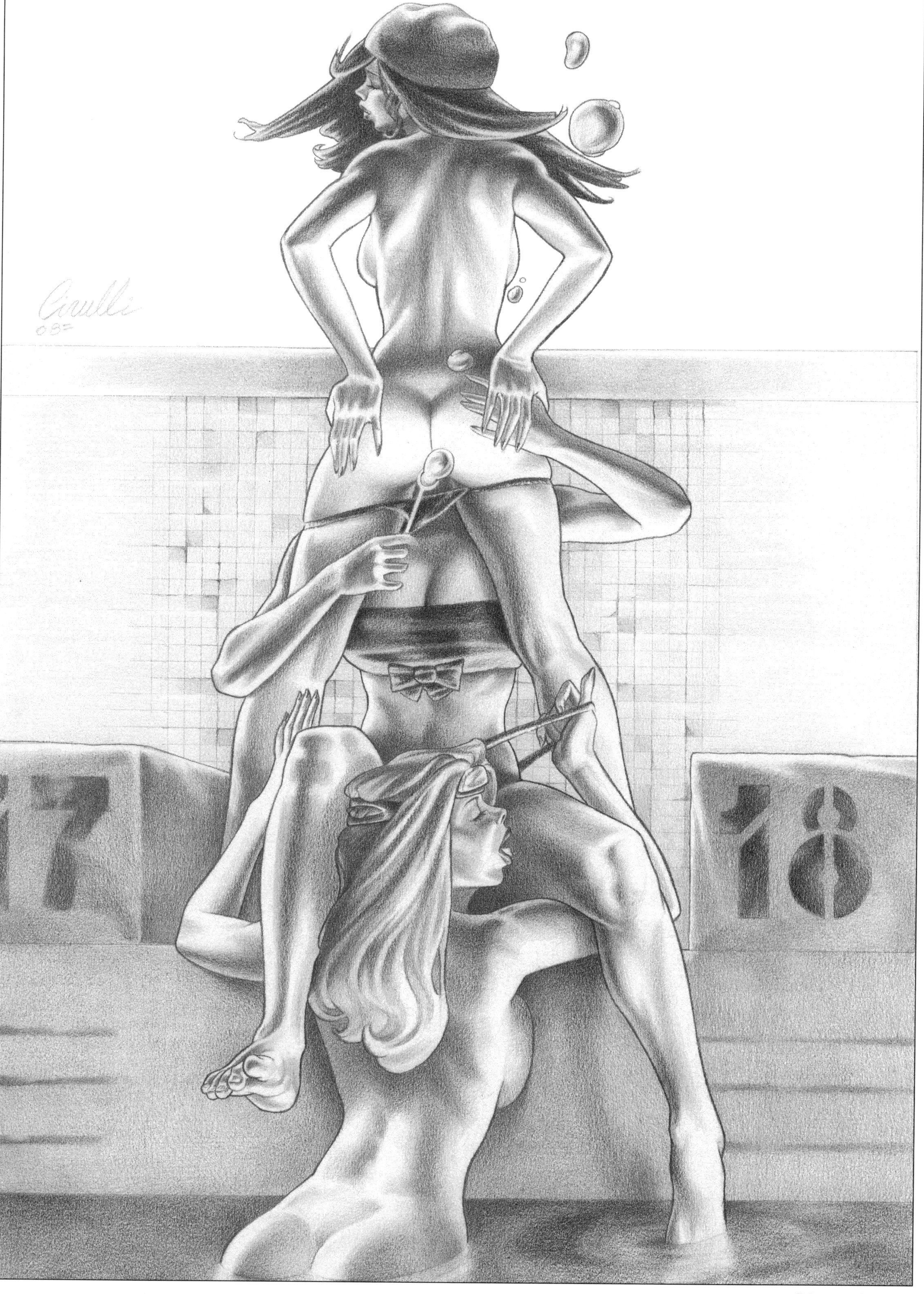

Diego Cirulli

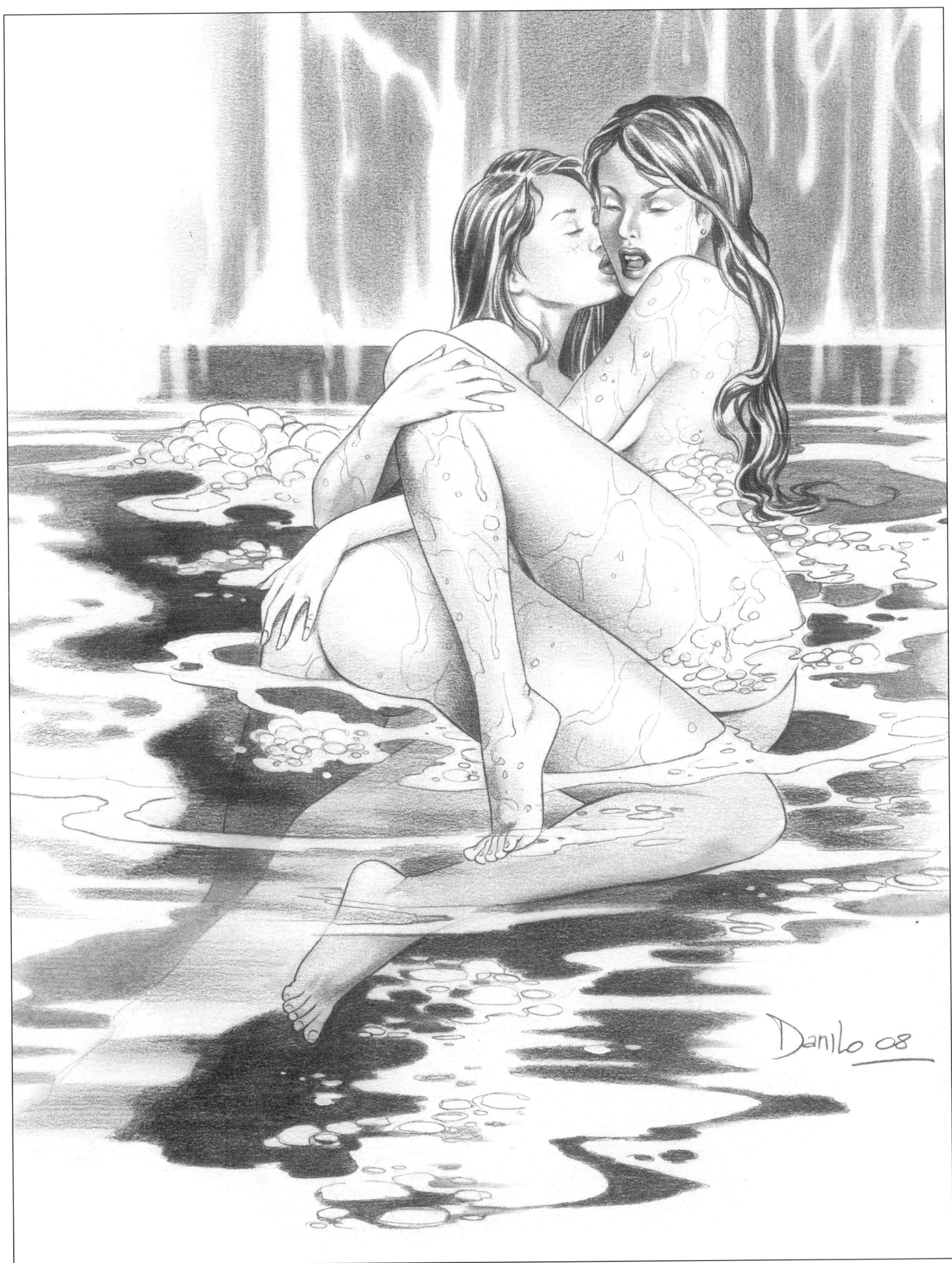

Danilo Guida

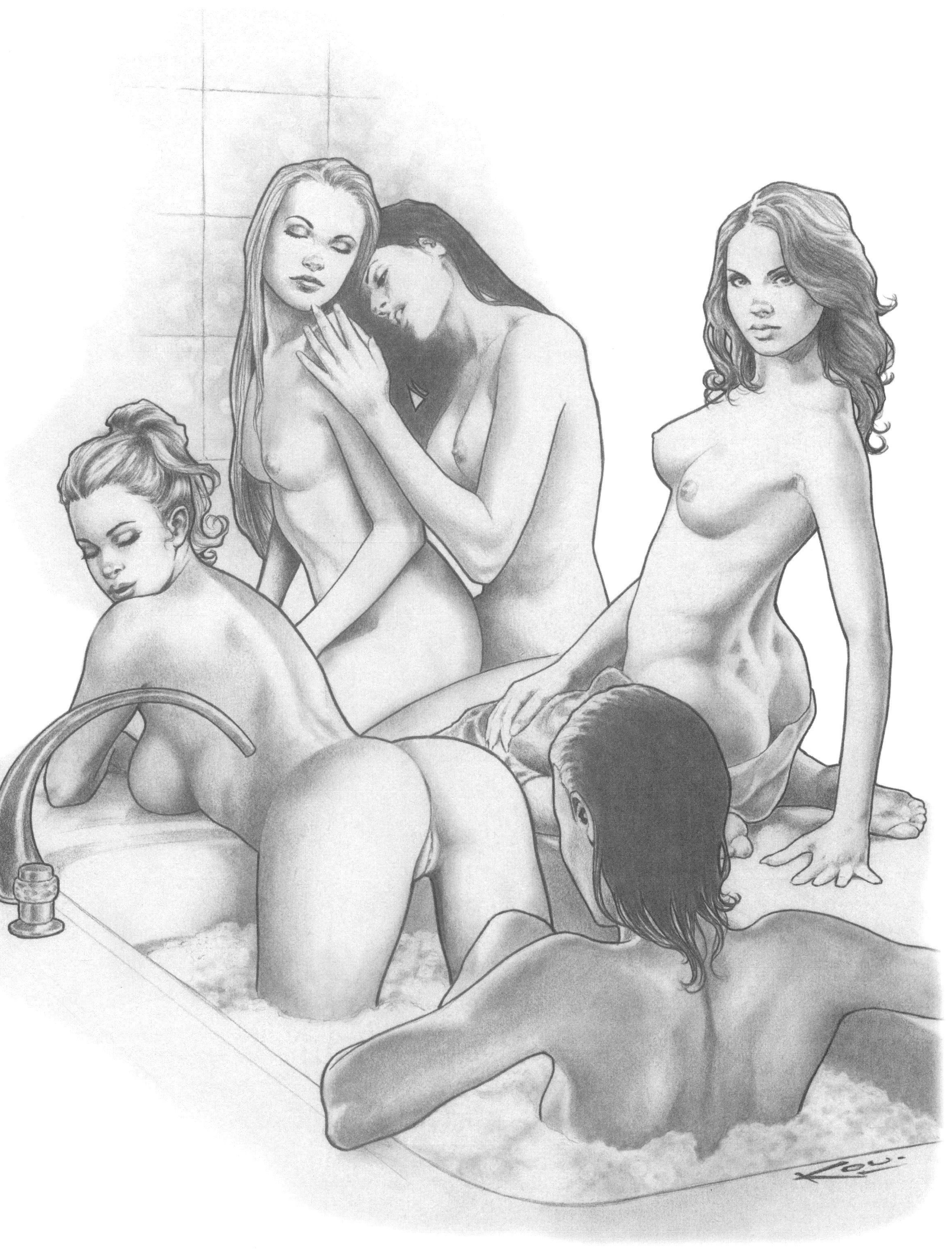

Pablo Kousovitis

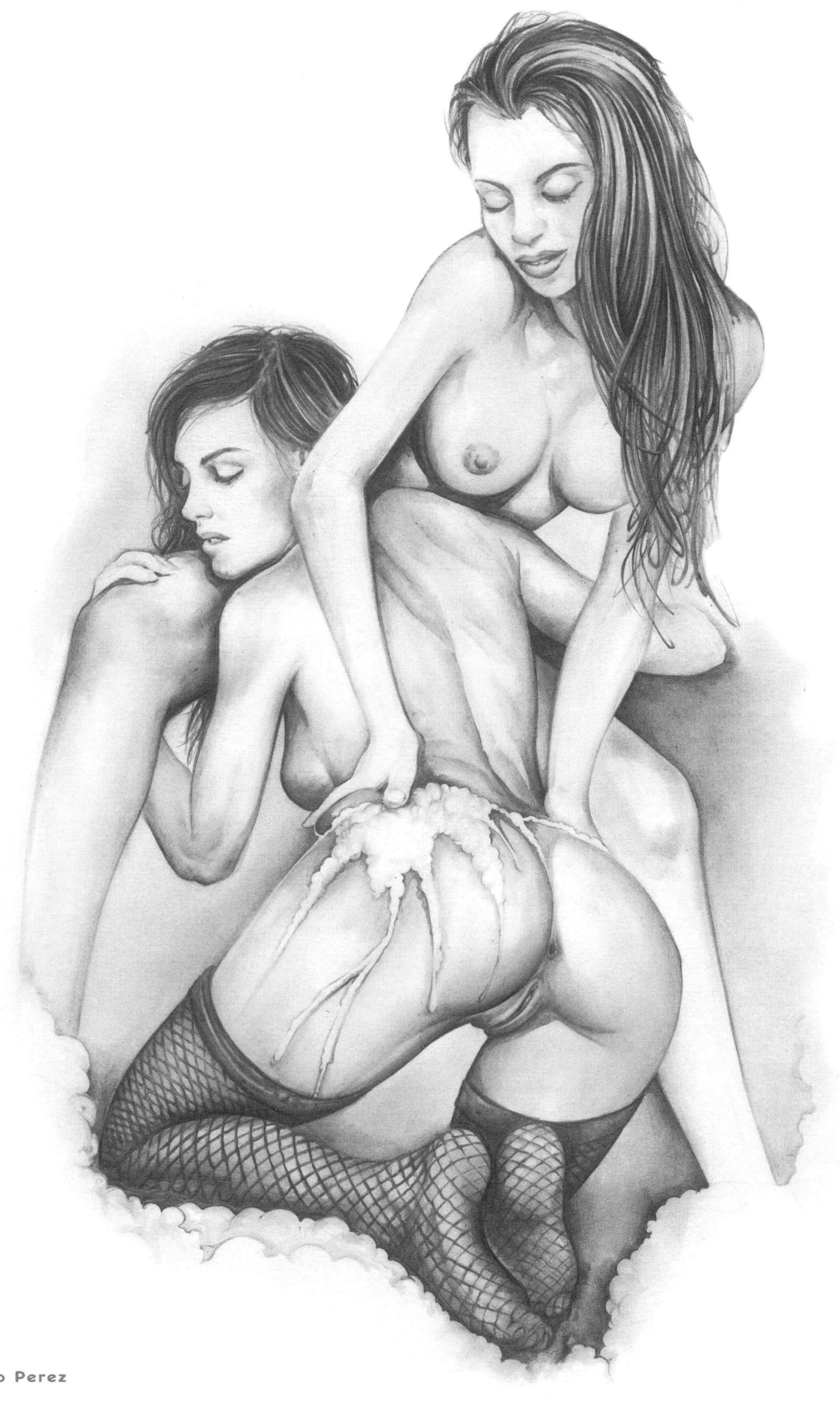

Aldo Perez

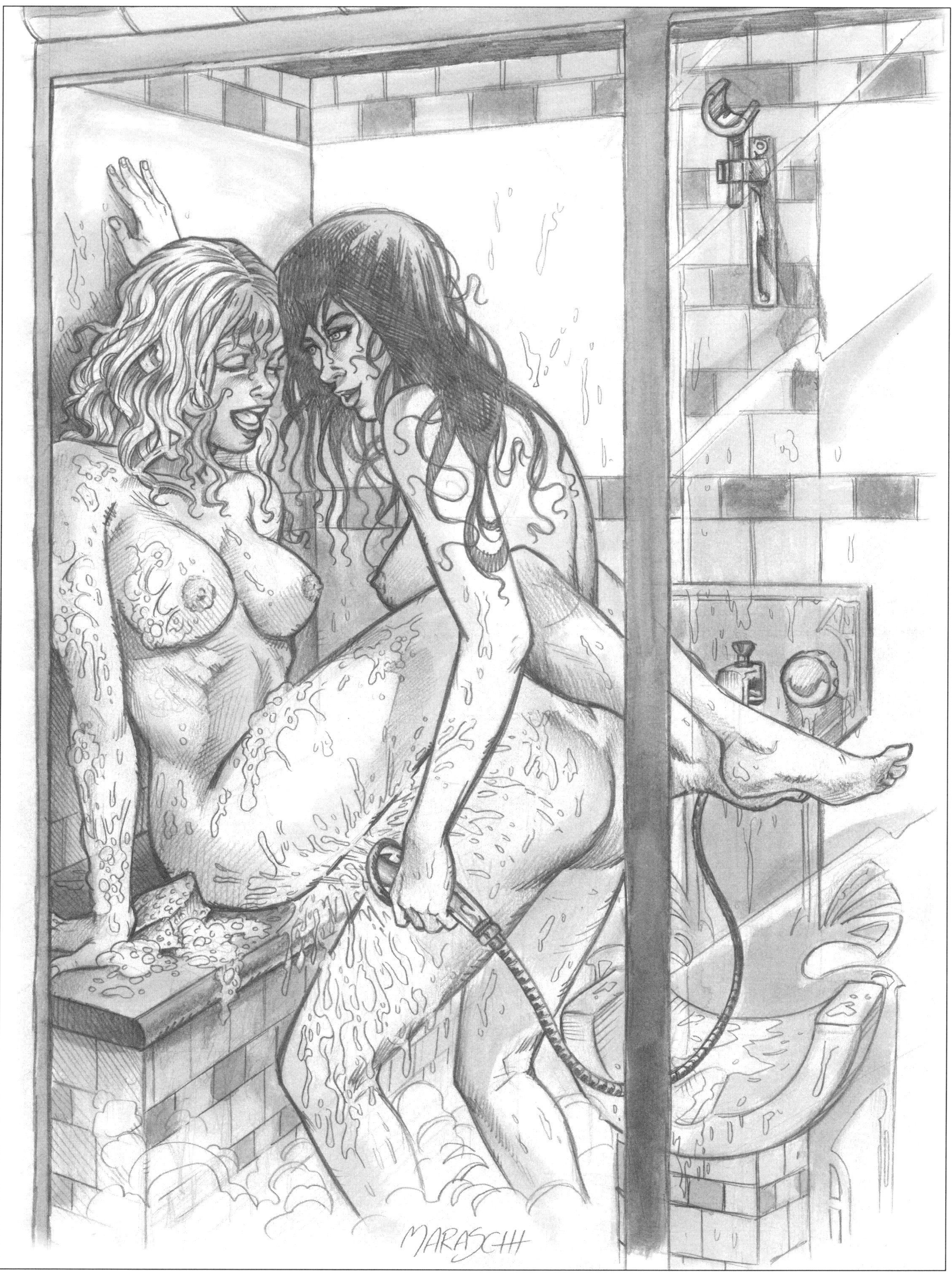

Anibal Maraschi

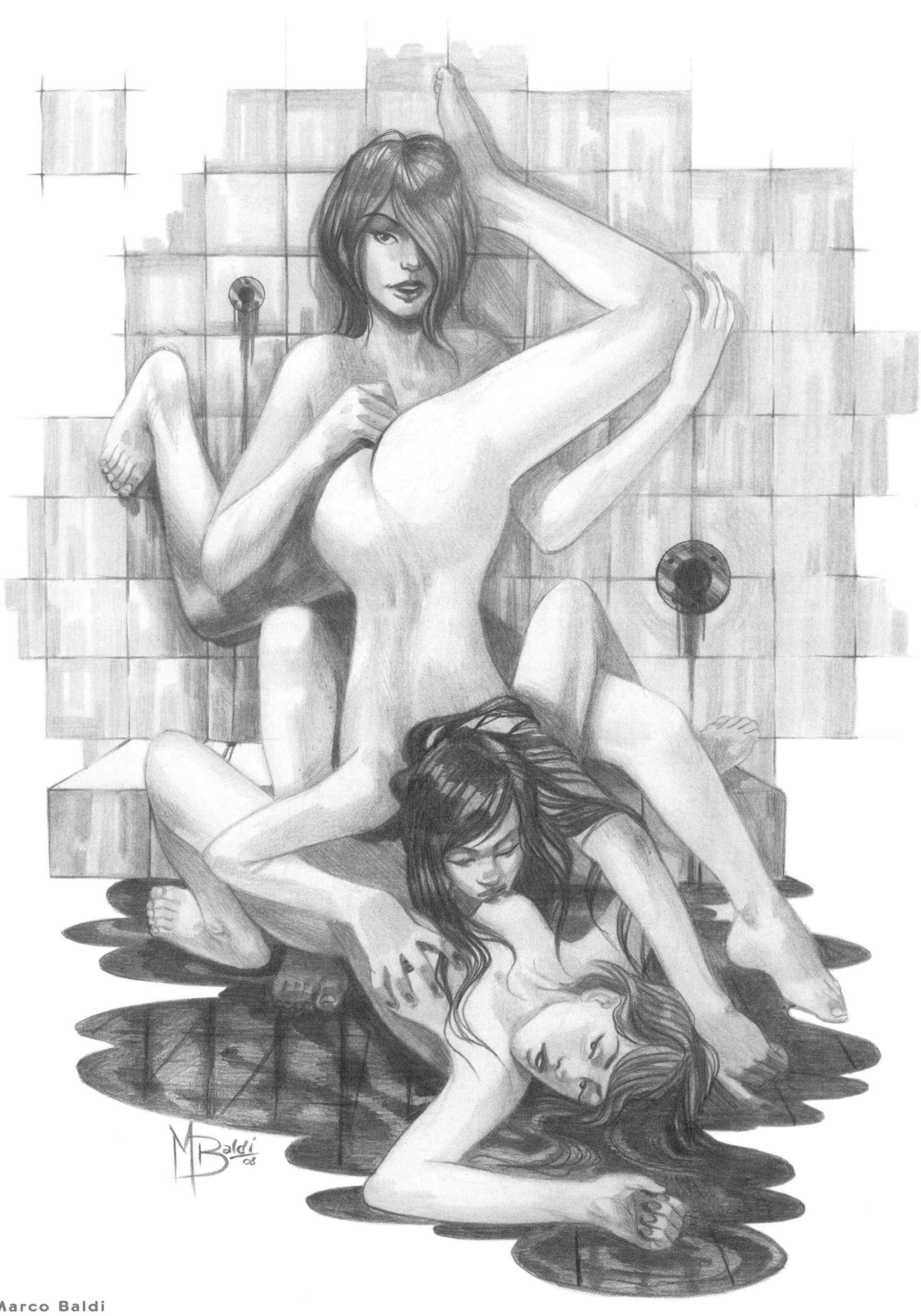

Marco Baldi

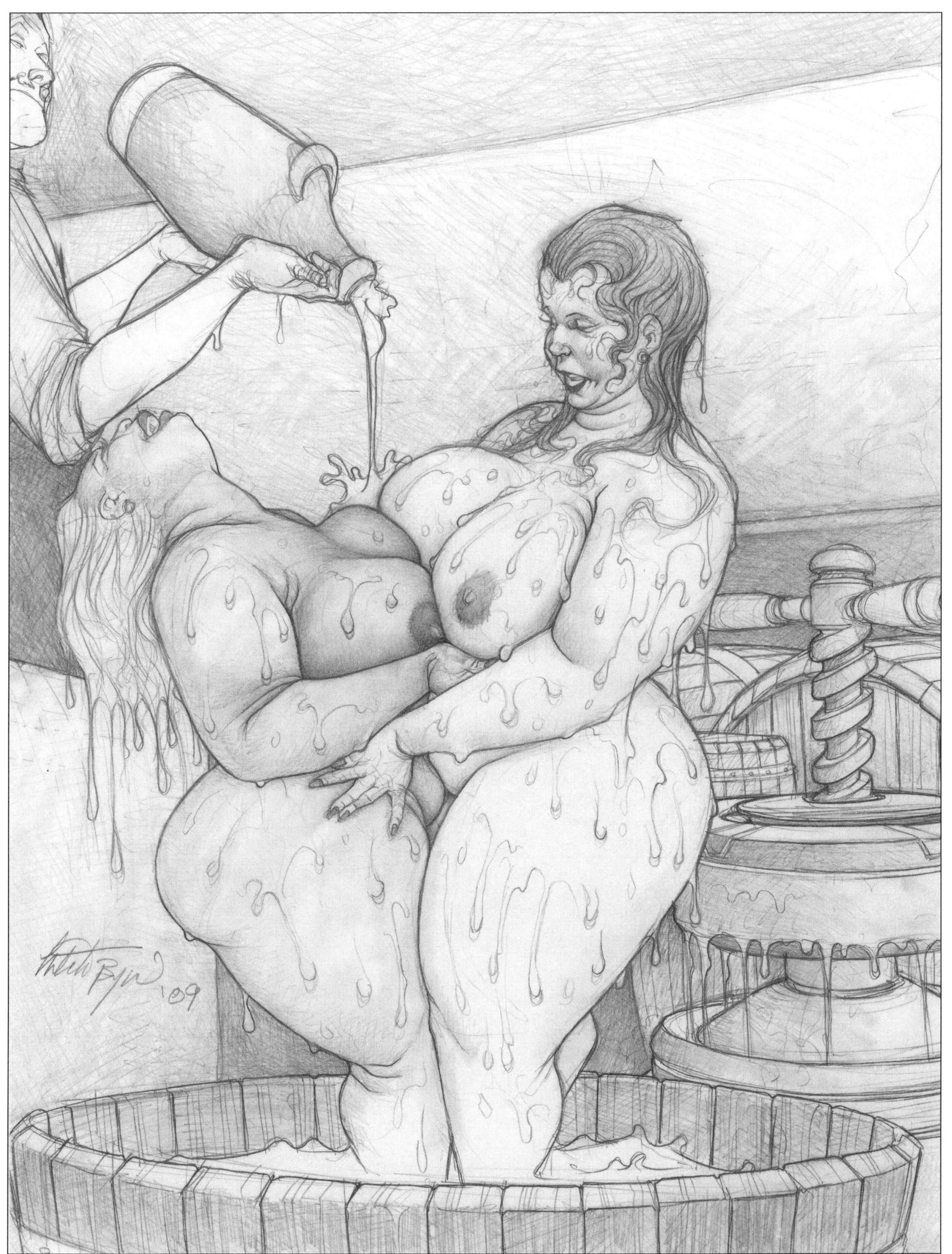

Mitch Byrd

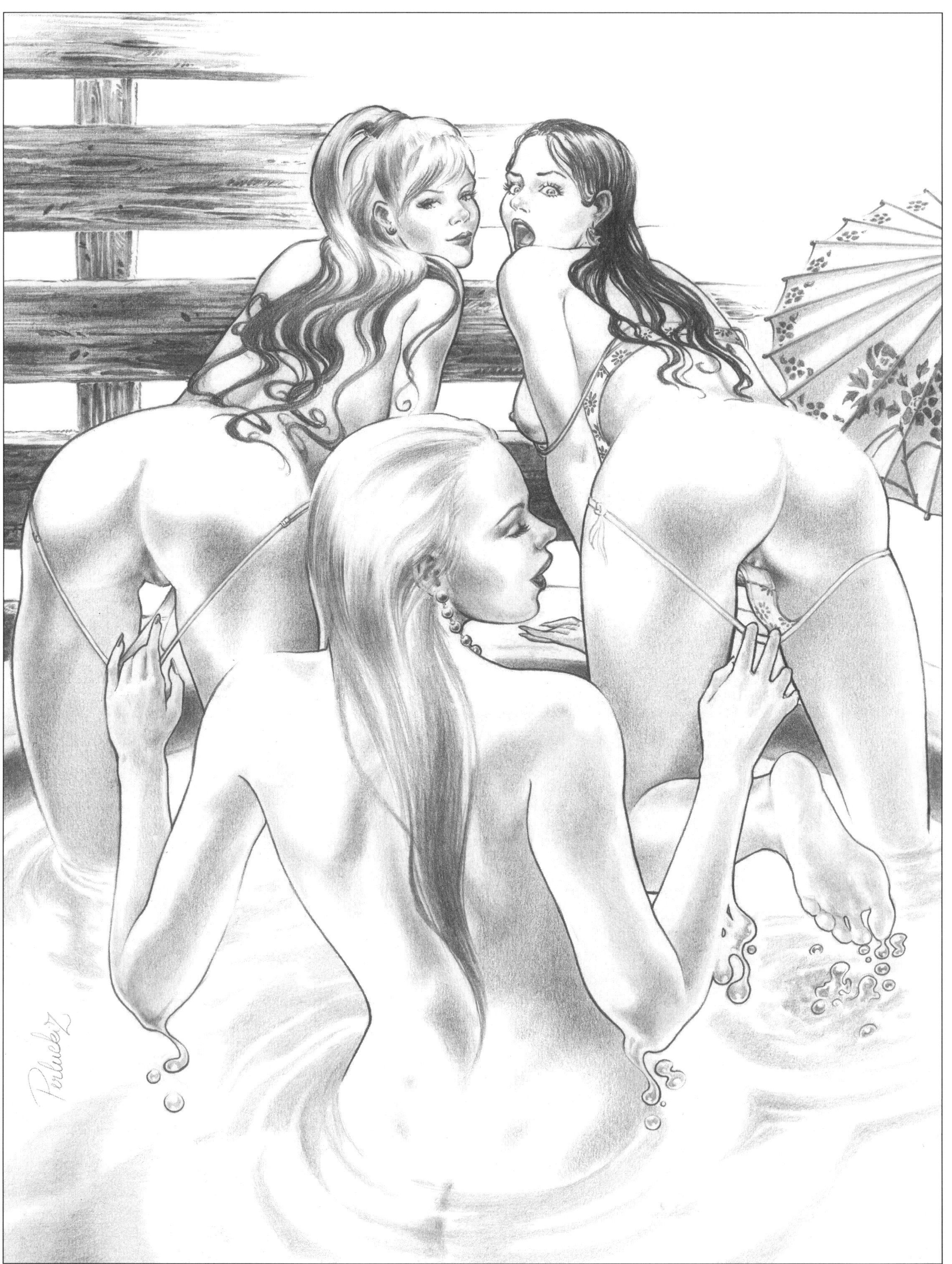

Perla Pilucki

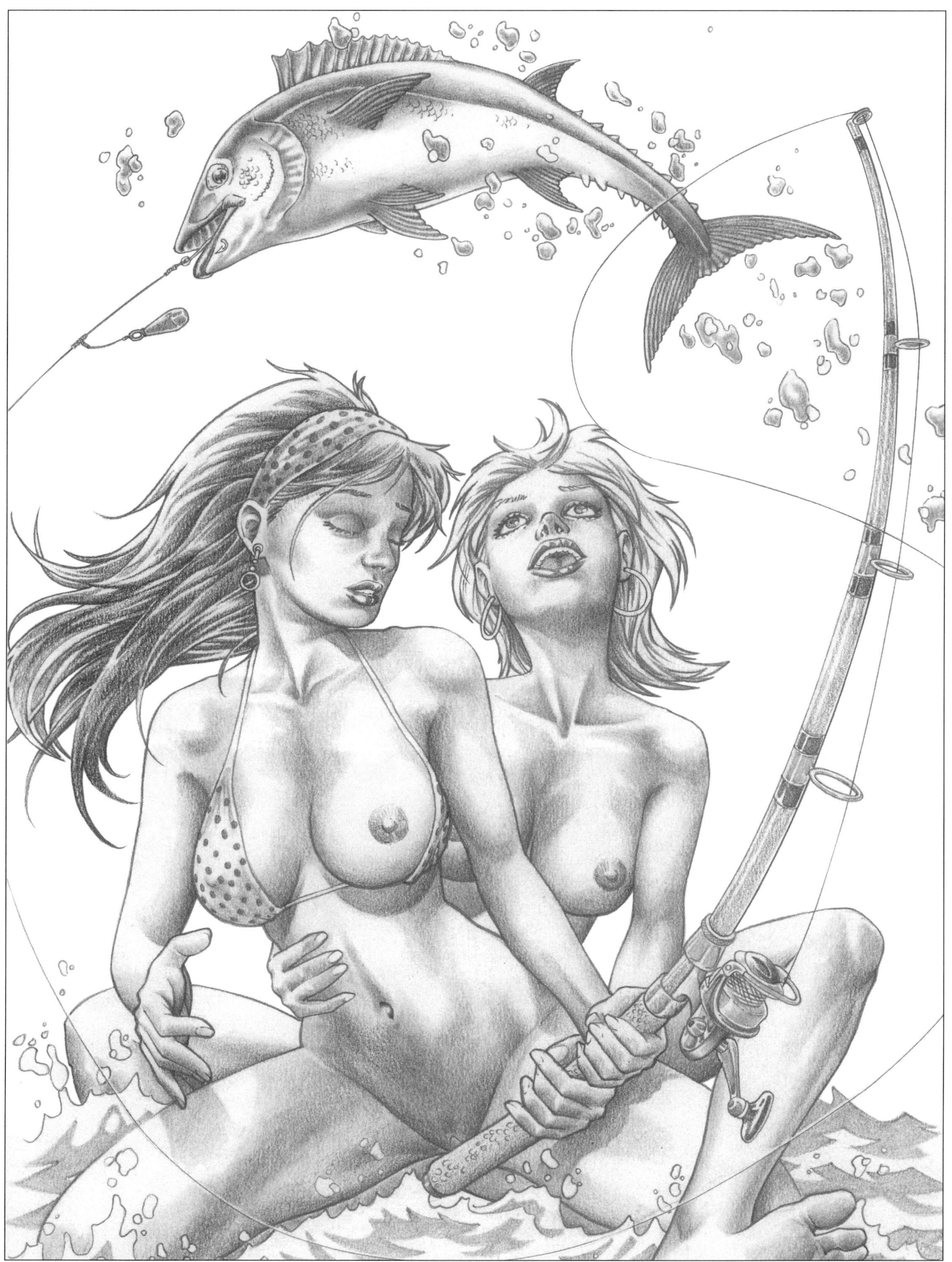

Emiliano Urdinola

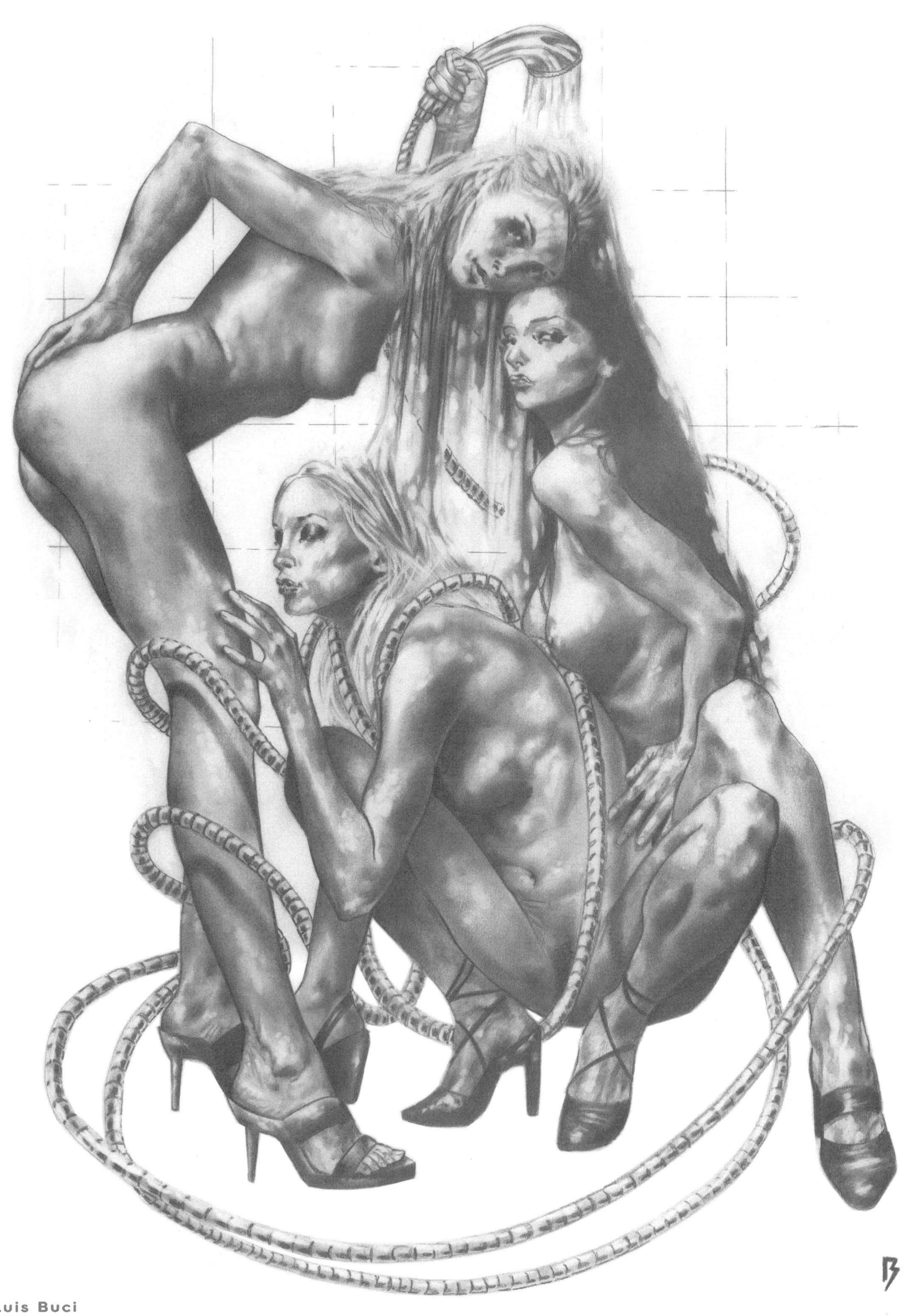

Luis Buci

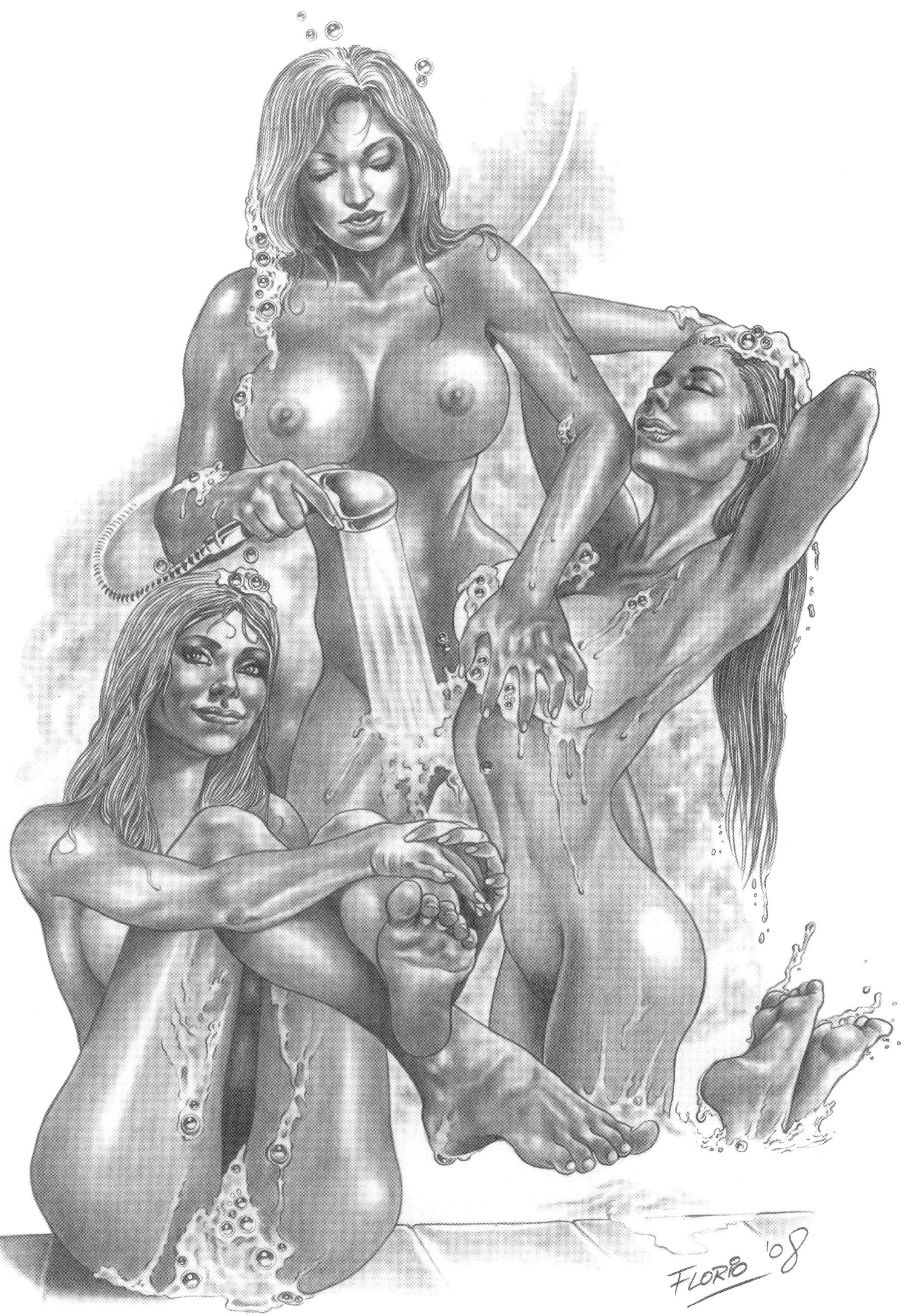

Diego Florio

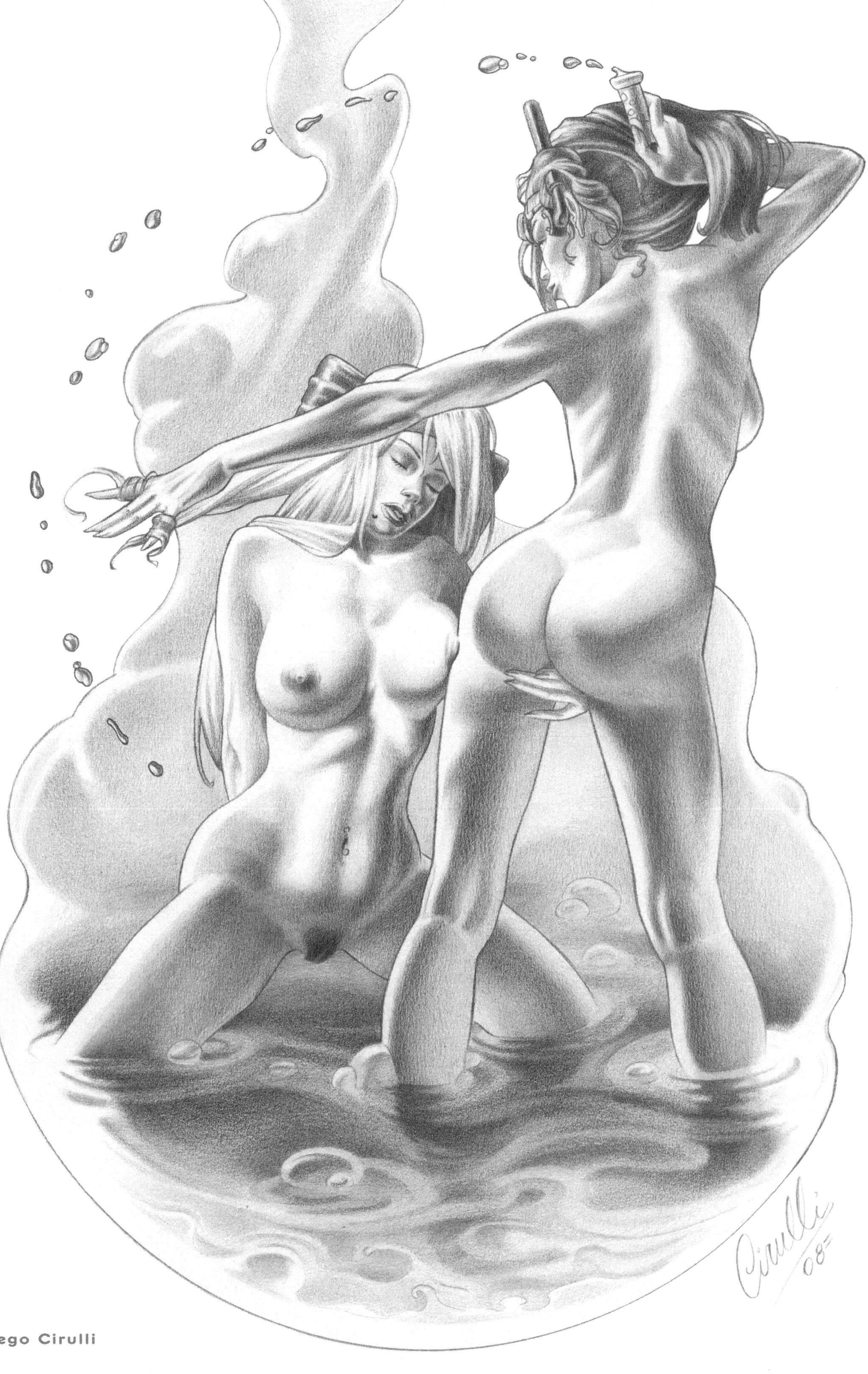

Diego Cirulli

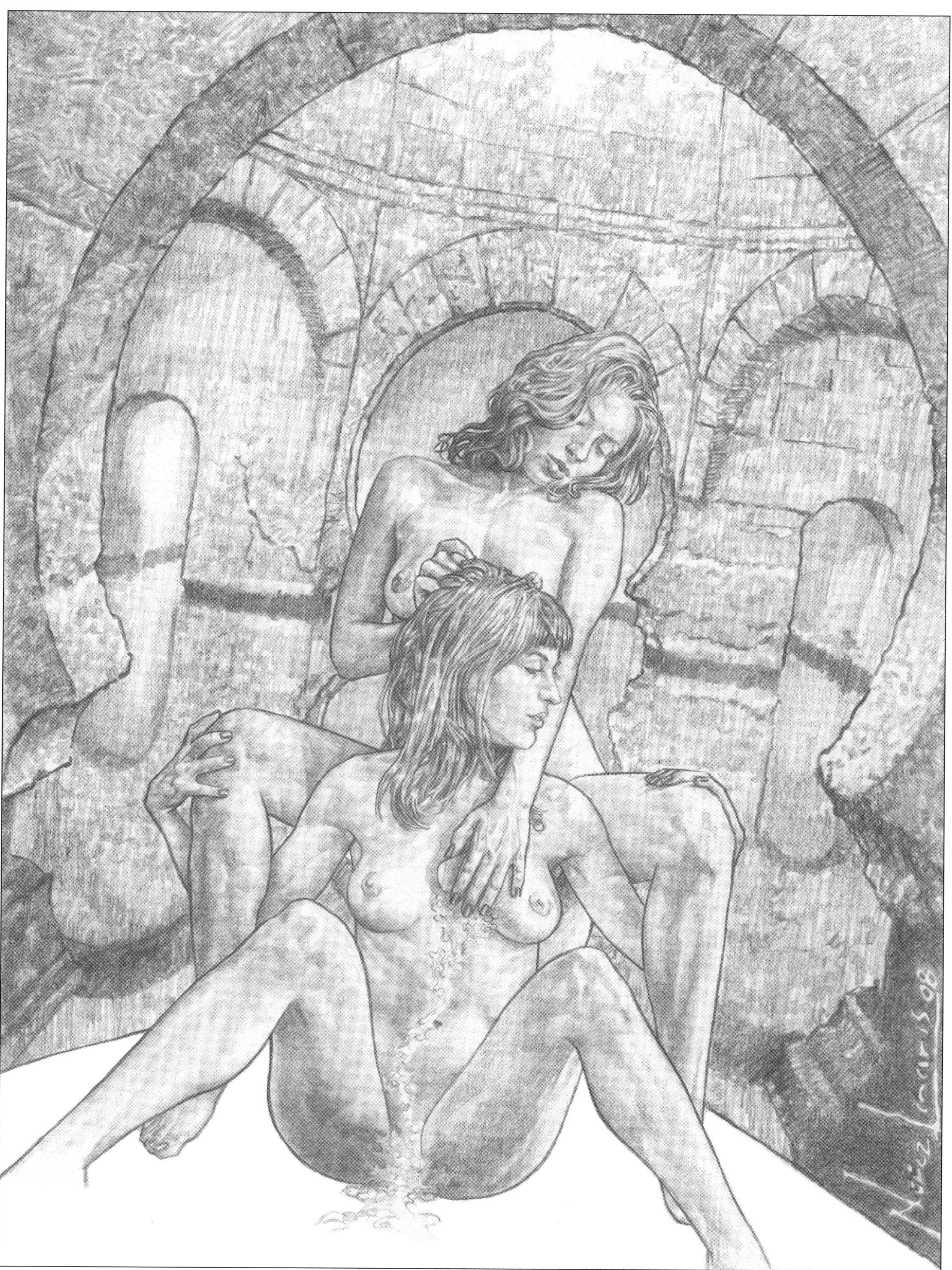

Juan Lencina

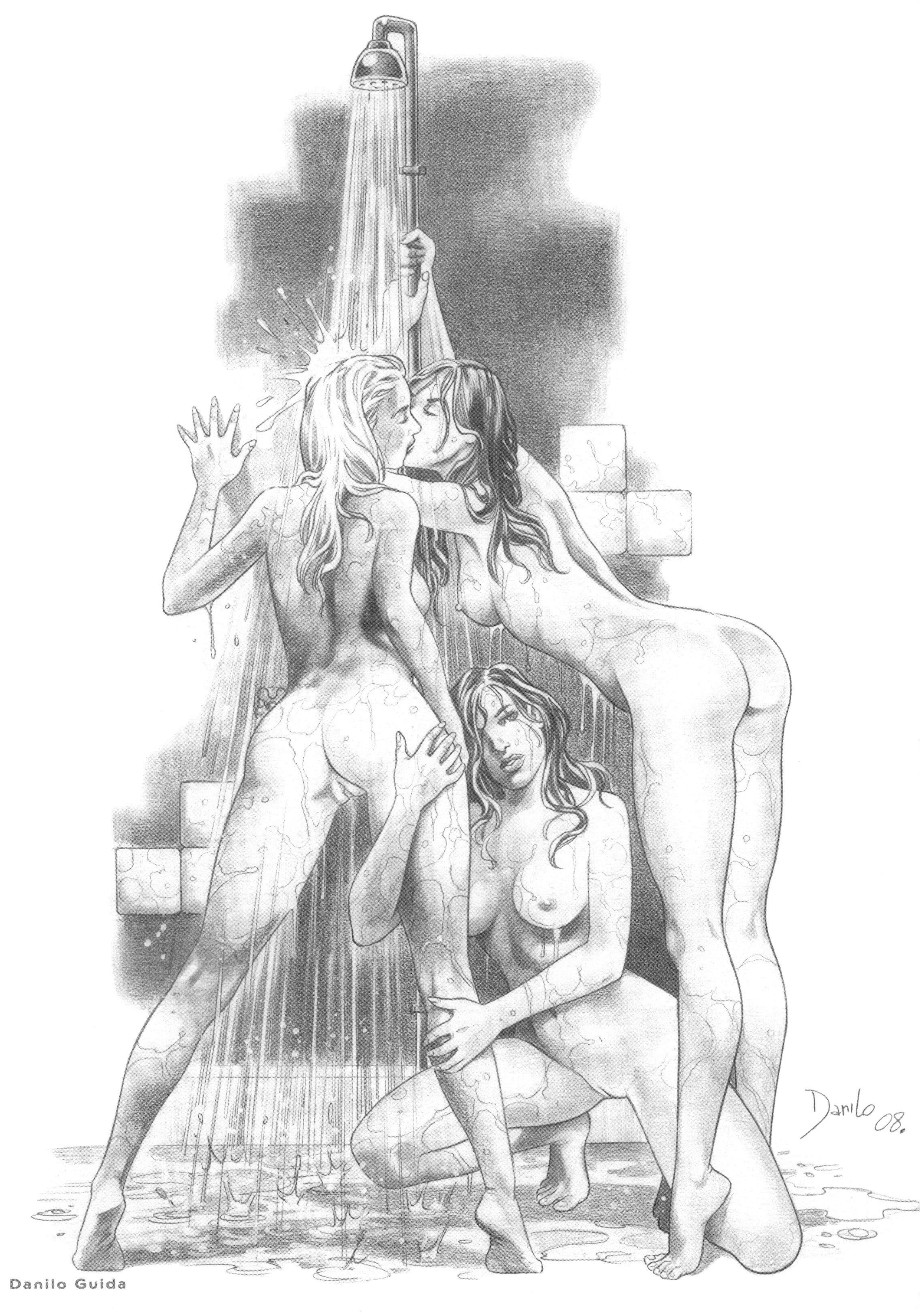

Danilo Guida

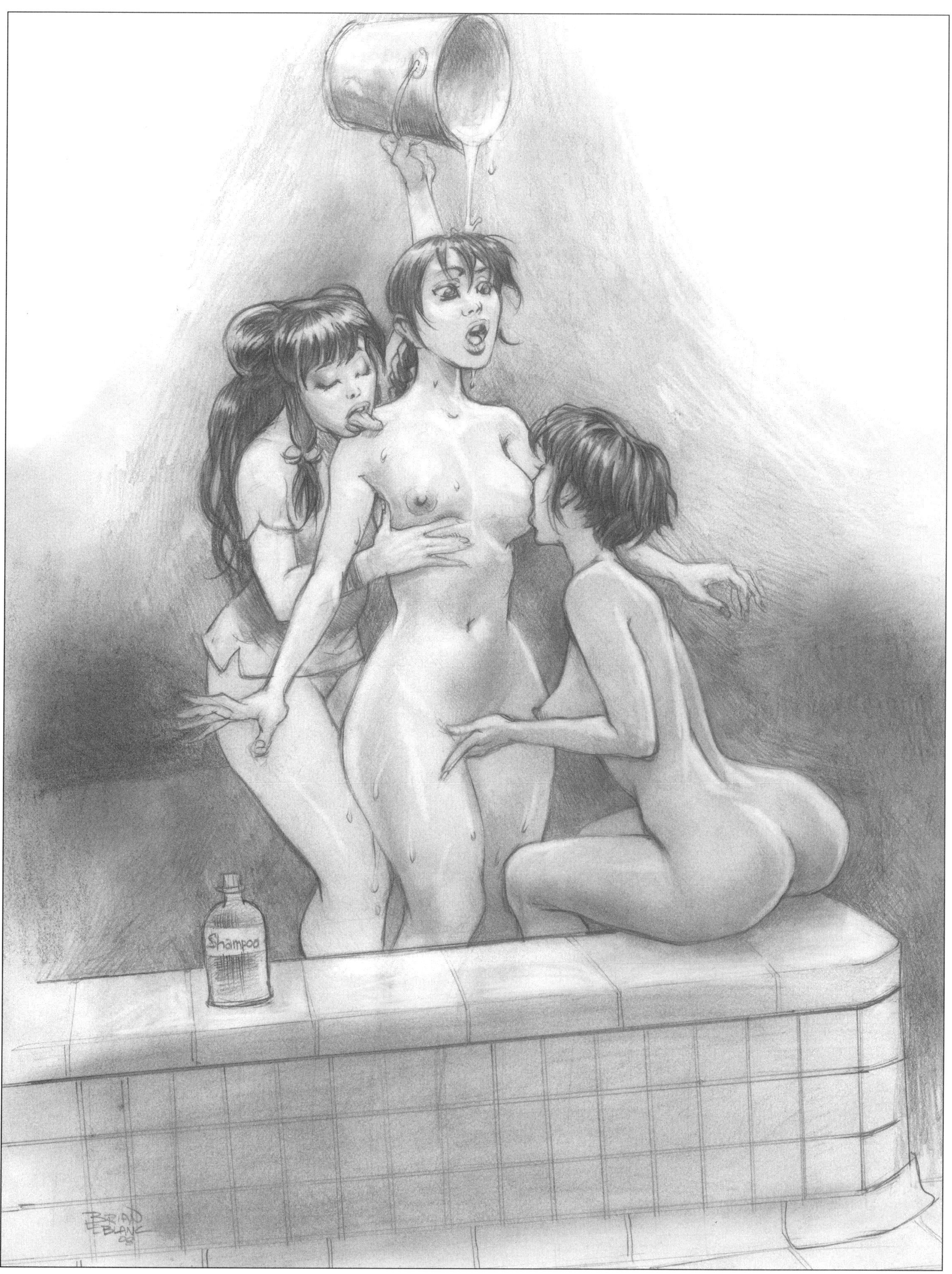

Brian LeBlanc

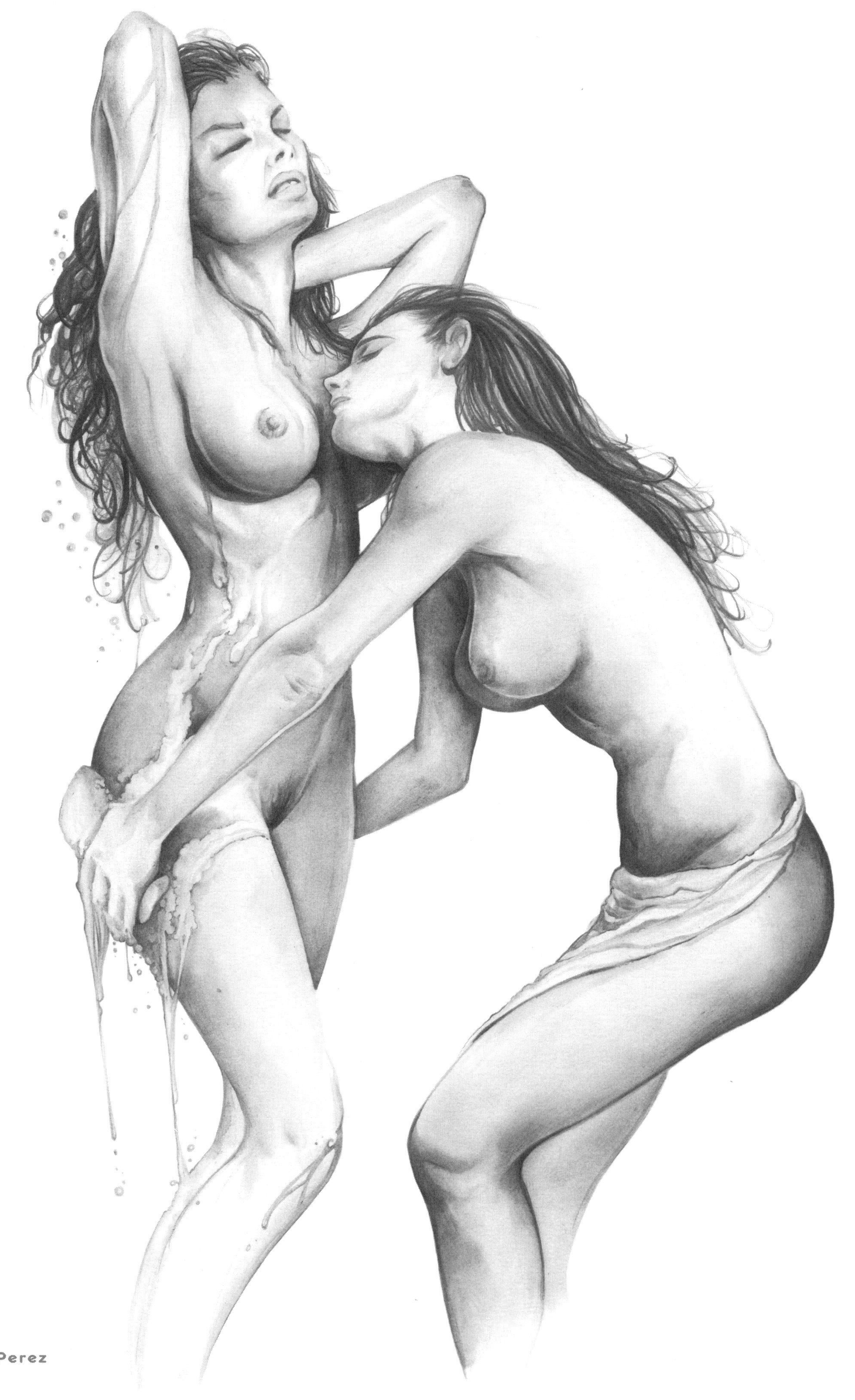

Aldo Perez

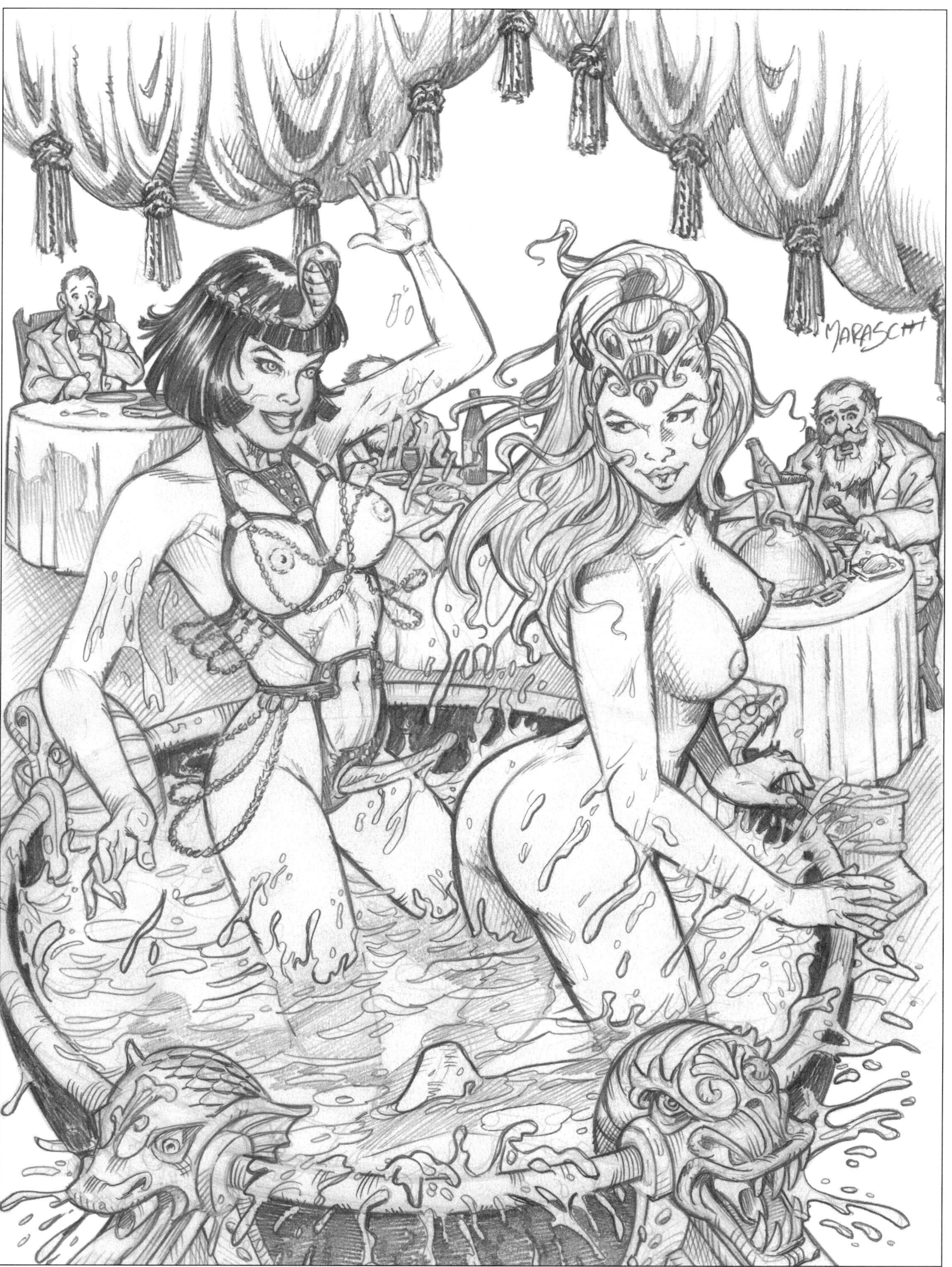

Anibal Maraschi

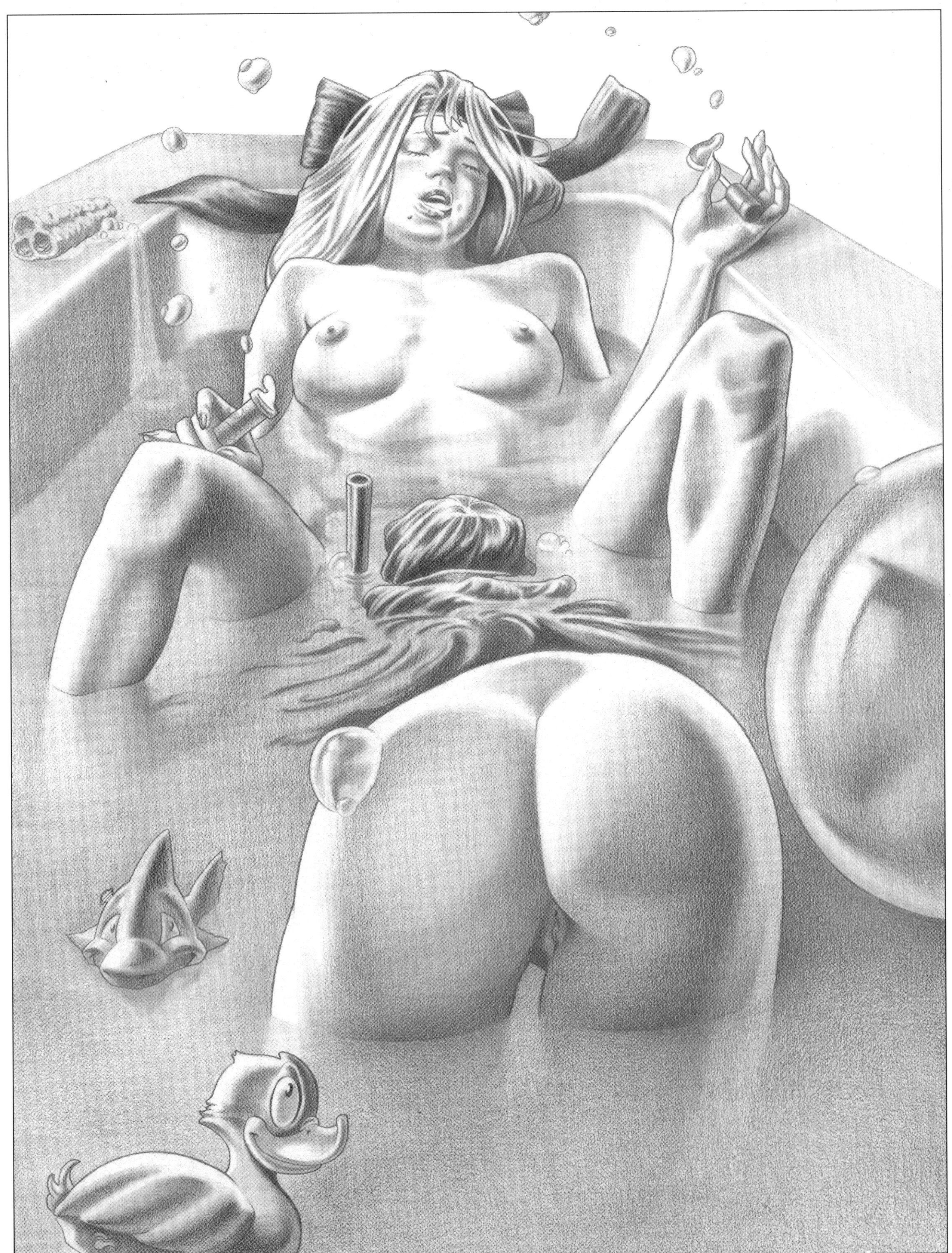

Diego Cirulli